Humorous Monologues and Dramatic Scenes

Belle Marshall Locke

Humorous Monologues and Dramatic Scenes

PRICE, 25 CENTS

Walter H. Baker & Co., Boston

Humorous Monologues

And Dramatic Scenes

By BELLE MARSHALL LOCKE
And Others

BOSTON
WALTER H. BAKER & CO.

Humorous Monologues

At the Market

Monologue for a Lady

By Belle Marshall Locke

At the Market

Good-morning, Mr. Blake. (*To dog.*) Lie down, Rover. Yes, this is my first trip to market, and I do hope I shan't appear too verdant. One of my college friends sent me a dear little book, bound in pale blue, with for-get-me-nots all over the cover, and the title was " Cooking for Two." Wasn't that the *dearest* title? What's that? It may prove so? I am sure it will, and I was so fascinated by the chapter on "Dainty Lunches" that I told Charlie I would not have a maid in the house, for I could hardly wait to try those recipes. Oh, no, he never has indigestion, at least he never had it until last night. I fried some cheese, and somehow it was stringy. Charlie said he felt as if he had been eating elastic bands.

Now, I really do not know a great deal about buying meat and vegetables, but that is one of the essentials of housekeeping—to do your own marketing—and I'm going to learn.

Mama had me excused from cooking school, for I was not strong enough to do much outside work and keep up my practice on the mandolin. I do just love a mandolin, don't you, Mr. Brown?

How much are those radishes a pound? Oh, you sell them by the bunch? Well, they are more attractive in that way— look almost like a bouquet, at a distance. (*Whistles to dog.*) Rover, come here, sir! Lovely dog, isn't he? That celery looks nice and green. How do you sell it? That seems high, when the tops are useless. Well, I'll take four bunches. I think that will be enough, allowing for waste. No, I'm afraid of oysters, since I have read so much about the typhoid germs. I went to a lecture last week, and I've felt creepy ever since. That man talked about germs, and the responsibility of serving food, until I was real nervous. He said that the lives of the family were often in the hands of the cook. I had a whole shelf full of canned goods, but I gave them to the washer-woman. Oh, yes, the lecturer had something to sell, and a woman served it to the ladies in the audience. The name of it is " Live Forever." It is lovely with stewed prunes and whipped cream, but Charlie doesn't fancy it somehow—said he shouldn't want to live forever if he had to be fed on that. He is so finnicky about his food, it is rather discouraging, sometimes. I bought a five-pound package of that cereal, and I don't know how I'll ever use it up.

Ugh, aren't those cranberries sour! They look better than they taste. What's in this tub? Sweet pickles? I just love pickles. These are delicious. How good of you to keep them out like that, so your customers can help themselves. When I asked Charlie where I should trade—for meats and vegetables, you know—he told me I had better come here. He is quite diplomatic, papa says, and he said he did not want you to think he had any hard feelings because he beat you for alderman. Every one can't hold office, you know, and you certainly were not to blame because Charlie has such a host of friends. He's generous, too, for I saw him give lame Mike— that man that lost his leg on the railroad, you know, ten dollars a while ago. He said, "If you feel like voting for me, old man, you'll find my name on the ballot." Never asked him to do it, but just spoke in that nice, quiet way. He knew Mike needed the money, and he didn't want to embarrass him, you see.

My! is that striking ten? Now, Mr. Blake, what do you think would be nice to have for meat on Thursdays? You see I am going to have fowl on Sunday, and Monday it will be easy to serve the chicken's remains in a fricassee. That settles Monday, and the cook book says to "have a roast on Tuesday, as the maid will iron and there will be a good fire." I send our laundry out, but I shall follow the rule given, just the same. Wednesday I can serve cold meat from the roast, or chops. Don't you think that chops—mutton, lamb, or pork, are popular? I thought so. Then comes Thursday, and that's a puzzling day, for I'm going to have fish Fridays, and chowder Saturdays; but Thursday —— Good-morning, Mrs. Spicer. Lovely day, isn't it? Going to rain? Yes, I noticed it as I came off the porch, and went back to change my hat. I had on that little poke lingerie affair, but I don't want to get it wet, for they are never so pretty after they are washed, do you think so? I'm glad to see that you come to this market, too, for every one says you are a model housekeeper. Charlie has been doing the marketing this last week, while we were getting settled. Yes, it is a pretty place, and I want my husband to love his home. That's why I am doing my own work. I'm going to have a woman come in and sweep and do the cleaning. I have a little girl come in every day to wash my dishes. I give her twenty-five cents every week, and I don't grudge it, either, for they are awfully poor and need the money. Certainly, don't let me detain you. I haven't a minute to spare, myself.

Oh, Mrs. Spicer! Just one moment. Would you be willing to write a paper for the club, next week? Just something short and to the point. The subject given is " How to better our Homes." I'm writing on " The Duties of a Young Housekeeper." Oh, yes, I see. Of course, if you are going to have company, I won't urge you. I'm expecting visitors myself, but—well, if she isn't the rudest woman I ever saw ! Walked right off when I was talking ! Her belt has slipped up at the back, and her dress isn't fastened behind, but I won't tell her of it. That waist was on the fifty cent bargain counter at Moulton and Hutton's last week, I saw it myself.

Well, Mr. Blake, I am surprised to see a woman like Mrs. Spicer, with all the money they've got, buying liver and bacon. I was expecting the very best steak, and possibly mushrooms; but you can't tell by the amount of money a person has what they have to eat at home. Certainly, don't let me keep you from other customers. A market is perfectly fascinating to me, and I like to look around and learn all I can. You don't mind? Thank you, I thought you wouldn't. (*To dog.*) Rover, come here. You mustn't poke your nose into things, like that. There, lie down, or I shan't take you, next time. I declare if that clerk isn't cheating Mrs. Doe. I heard her call for two pounds of veal, and I was looking straight at the scales when he weighed it, and it didn't tip but a pound and three quarters. Mr. Blake, pardon me, but I think that you should know that that boy is either careless or dishonest. He gave Mrs. Doe a pound and three quarters of veal, when she called for two pounds. I heard her give the order and saw him, with my own eyes, weigh it. I thought you should know it, for if help cheat one person they will another, and it's the little things that count in business. That tripe looks nice. Is it pickled? We prefer it to fresh. How much is it? Why, I didn't realize it was so cheap. I remember my little book says it is very healthful, and now I recall it, I was at Martin's Ferry one summer, and the hired man was just getting up from a fever. The doctor said he could have tripe, and it didn't hurt him a bit. I'll take four pounds, and that will allow for shrinkage, for it does frizzle up so when it's cooked, doesn't it? I don't mind asking you questions, you see, for I know how intimate you and Charlie are, being so closely allied in politics.

Can you send the tripe and celery, right away? Thank you. Oh, yes, we like the house very much. Of course, I have been accustomed to a large place and servants, but I always said I would never marry for money, and I kept my word. Why it can't be possible that it is striking eleven! How time does fly when one is busy.

Oh, no, we don't intend to run an account. Pay as you go, is my motto. Why, how funny that sounds! I didn't realize I was rhyming. Speaking of poetry, reminds me of your daughter, Addie. She was our class poet. I am so sorry her husband has failed in business. I intended to go right over and sympathize with her as soon as I heard about it, but was too busy just then. Tell her not to feel badly or sensitive over it. We shall all treat her just as well, and she isn't to be expected to shoulder all her husband's faults. Yes, that's the right change, only that dime is all flattened out. Looks as if some boy had put it on the car track, doesn't it? You may think I'm fussy, but I do like good, clean looking silver and fresh bills in my purse. Thank you. (*Whistles.*) Rover! Rover! where are you? What's that you're saying? He has eaten two pounds of steak off that bench? What a preposterous story! Rover never climbed on that bench and ate that meat in this world! What's that you say, boy? You saw him? Well, I must say you are in good business, hanging 'round a market and spying on a dog! Why aren't you at school?

What's that you say, Mr. Blake? You'll have to charge the steak? What? You don't mean to tell me that you are going to charge for a morsel of meat that dog picked up?—If he did, which I very much doubt. It's business? I don't consider it so, at all. We are giving you our trade, and a few mouthsful of meat compared to that is simply nothing. It certainly is not worth disputing over, and I shall not pay for it without consulting Charlie. I felt all the time we were doing a foolish thing to trade here, when Mr. Porter's market is much larger, and patronized by the best people in town. You needn't expect me again. I have too much self-respect to patronize a man who was so stingy as to even speak of a bit of meat a dog might eat, when there is more of it lying around than you will ever sell. But some people would rather have anything spoil on their hands than see a dumb creature eat it. Come, Rover, come here, sir! Where has he gone? Put down that bone! You shan't eat a mouthful of meat in this place!

I don't wonder you do not succeed in politics, Mr. Blake, if you count every penny like that. It's your fault that you have lost a good customer, and I'll have Charlie go to law, before he shall pay one cent for that meat! Bear that in mind! Rover, come here! [*Exit.*

Making a Mason

Descriptive Monologue for a Lady

By Belle Marshall Locke

Making a Mason

Mrs. Dillydally was lonely, very lonely. Not that this was unusual, for during the last six months of her three years of wedded bliss (?) Algernon, or "Algie," as she called him in the old, happy days, had joined four secret societies and a club. To-night he would become a member of a very secret order—five in all.

She had counted them over on the fingers of her left hand, including the thumb; then she went to the window and gazed through the flying snowflakes across the street. A young girl, with her sweetheart, was coming down the steps of the house opposite. They were evidently going to the theatre, for she carried an opera glass bag, and the wind, blowing her cape open, displayed a dainty evening gown. How tenderly he re-arranged the refractory garment as they went down the street laughing. It brought the old joyous days to her mind most vividly.

"I'd never know there was a theatre in the world, if I waited for him to take me!" she muttered, as she pulled down the shades and threw herself on the couch, for a good cry.

She had arranged the pillows in order to be as comfortable as possible, while she courted misery, when the door-bell rang. Hastily brushing away her tears and rearranging her side-combs, she flew to the door, eager to welcome any one who would break the monotony of a lonely evening. "Oh, Mrs. Cheeriton, I'm so glad to see you!" she exclaimed, dragging a laughing, little woman into the hall. "I actually believe you have saved me from suicide. Take your hat right off. Isn't it a beauty!—and say! you *did* get that lovely set of Silver Fox, down at Sellem's, didn't you? I saw them in the window and raved over them to Algernon, but that is all the good it did. It takes all his extra money now to join lodges. I can't go very much myself, for I must economize when those everlasting dues are always coming in. That's right, sit here. (*Motions for her to be seated right.*) I'm glad you brought

15

your work. I'll get mine, for I am just rushed with Christmas things, and these crocheted slippers hang on so, it seems as if I'd never finish this one. (*Sits and pantomimes crocheting.*) As I was saying, I don't go very much. Mrs. Gadabout was here to-day, teasing me to join the N. A. G. Club, but I couldn't afford it. I was sorry, for they do good, steady work."

"Too bad you can't get out more, dear," said Mrs. Cheeriton, with an odd, little laugh. "Don't you belong to a club of any sort?"

"Only 'The Jolly Set,' 'The Merry Wives,' The Ibsen Class, two whist clubs, one afternoon for 'Bridge,' and 'The Daughters of Delilah.' One must be seen among people once in a while, you know, but that husband of mine has a perfect mania for joining things—all secret orders, too, which I consider an outrage for a married man. He's taking in the Masons to-night."

"You mean the Masons are taking him in, my dear. I remember when Mr. Cheeriton joined them. It was a 'Blue' lodge the night he joined—so was he, both black and blue."

"Why, what in the world do you mean?" said Mrs. Dillydally, as she dropped her crochet work and allowed the hook to roll under the table. (*Pause.*)

"I wonder if you would feel a little less injured and more anxious, if I told you just what is going to happen to your husband to-night."

Mrs. Dillydally was on her feet in an instant.

"Do you know? Have you found out? Has he told you? I thought ——"

"Never mind what you thought, I know," said Mrs. Cheeriton, as she closed the door into the hall and looked behind the portières. "Dorothy Dillydally, there are blood-curdling events taking place in that hall to-night, and your husband is playing the leading part."

"For heaven sake tell me what you mean! Don't hesitate, for I am a woman of few words, and will never lisp it to a living soul. It is high time we women rose in our might, and demanded these secrets from a lot of stage struck—no, lodge struck men."

"That's just what I did, my dear, and I am going to tell you out of sympathy, poor little abused woman that you are! Don't I know too well what a woman suffers evening after evening alone, while her husband is off taking degrees—and there will be thirty-three of 'em, this time—make up your mind to that! Now listen. A few years ago my husband told me he was going to join the Masons that night. He belonged to every order under the sun then, and some that wouldn't bear the sun, and I couldn't see any probable stopping place unless I was wise enough to assert my rights. Of course, you have heard of the last straw and what it did to the camel's back? Well, I was the camel, and I balked good and hard. He came home early that evening, and if he had been getting ready for his own wedding, he would not have spent more time on his toilet. I was waiting in the library when he came downstairs, and I called him in. 'Charles Chesterfield Cheeriton,' I began, 'you are intending to join another secret order tonight.' 'Yes, love, the Masons. They are the oldest——' 'Never mind their age. I want to say right now that I will never live with you another day, if you're going to have a lot more secrets from me, your lawful, wedded wife. No, sir, unless you tell me everything about to-night's doings, I will leave this house, to-morrow!' 'For how long?' said he. 'Forever!' I replied, throwing his meerschaum pipe off the mantel on the hearth and stamping on it. 'Well, I'll see what can be done about it,' said he, turning to go. 'Possibly they won't mind one woman knowing,' and he turned the door knob. 'Wait!' I cried, with a real dramatic gesture. 'Swear to me that you'll tell me every blessed or unblessed thing that takes place at that asylum for be-knighted lunatics to-night,' and I seized what I thought was the Bible from the table, and administered the oath. Afterward, I found it was a new cook book, but I don't think he noticed the difference."

"Go on! go on!" cried Mrs. Dillydally. "Oh, won't I get even with Algernon!"

"Yes, you will—most women do get even," said Mrs. Cheeriton, solemnly. "Well, I sat up for him, and it was one o'clock when I heard him trying to use the latch-key. I flew to the door. What a sight I beheld!"

"Yes, yes, go on!"

"My husband stood before me, a wreck! I pushed him into a chair and examined his collar. The button-hole was burst! His necktie had two spots on it and was untied. One cuff button was gone, his shoes had been unlaced; there was a smut on his nose, a bloody cross on his forehead, and two bright spots on his left breast, that looked like the imprints of a sharp instrument."

" Heavens, what had happened ? "

" I pulled one shoe off and —— Oh, it is too awful to tell ! "

" Speak ! what was it ? "

" His stocking was on wrong side out.   I stood and looked at him a moment, then I said in icy tones: ' Well, begin.   You are now supposed to be at the door of that chamber of horrors.' "

" Go on ! "

" He was shaking with exhaustion, and I actually had to give him brandy before he could speak.   Every word he said is burned into my brain, and I will tell it to you.   ' When that door opened,' said he, ' the place was so full of sulphur, I nearly choked.   Fiends were dancing around a gridiron heated red hot, over a cauldron of living coals, which were fanned by chafing-dish aprons, made of lamb's skin, which those grinning demons wore.   They were the fire-worshipers and the name of their chief was " Zoroaster."   They made me salaam to the east, west and south, and when I asked them what the north had done, some one knocked me down, with a mallet.   Then they seized me, like an innocent calf, and branded me with their private brand, which is a square and compass.'   He moved uneasily, and said, ' That brand will never be effaced.   Before I had time to talk back, I was made to dance the " Highland Fling " on a cake of ice in my bare feet, after which I was thrown on a blanket and came down on a mattress, fifteen feet, the mattress being filled with tacks, ends up.' "

Mrs. Dillydally was white and trembling, but Mrs. Cheeriton went steadfastly on.   " At this ' point,' my husband was so agitated he had to quench his thirst, and proceeded.   ' I had barely time to recover my breath from the last at-" tack," when a goat rushed in and played ball with me.   That bewhiskered beast would toss me into the air, when a ghostly being, with a skull for a head, batted me back to the pitcher !

" ' Talk about ball playing !   That goat could give Cy Young points, and sharp ones, too, on the game.   Then I was made to carry bricks and mortar up a ladder six times.   The ladder had thirty-three rungs in it, and the last time up every bit of that thing fell into inch pieces, and I was precipitated into a bottomless pit, or so it seemed as I was whirling through space ; but finally I struck a landing, which proved to be a floor, paved with skulls and cross bones.   Here I was made to take a big pinch of red pepper for snuff, and sit ten minutes with a smutty, old clothes-pin, on my nose, so I couldn't sneeze, while a human bat painted a cross on my forehead in red hot blood.'

"Would you believe it, my dear, I couldn't stand it to hear another word, but came so near fainting, he had to stop; he said the rest was so bad he could not describe it without shedding tears. 'Give me the sign,' I said, 'and I'll be satisfied. I want the next Mason I meet to understand that I know as much as he does.' 'You do, my dear, and a great deal more.' Then he rose from his chair with difficulty, and kicked as high as he could with his right foot, winked with his left eye, then, with his right, put his thumbs on his ears and wagged his fingers. 'If you do this,' he said, 'no Mason will fail to recognize you.'"

Mrs. Dillydally was crying. Finally she sprang to her feet and cried, "Murderers! I'll telephone for the police."

"No use, my dear, the City Marshal is a Mason."

"Think of the agony my husband is suffering this very moment!" she sobbed. "What shall I do! what shall I do!"

"Take my advice and be calm. Get to work and make ready for his return, for I assure you that your house should be transformed into a private hospital. Bring in the kitchen table and put these articles on it. You will need to use them, at once. A bottle of arnica, mustard plaster, box of vaseline, antiphlogistine, bandages, medicated cotton, surgeon's plaster and skin food. Have you all these remedies?"

"Yes," she moaned.

"Well, cheer up, it will soon be over; and I will run home and fix a hot lunch for Charles. He will be worn out. It is so hard to 'work' a whole evening, as they do, and it certainly is nerve-racking to raise a Mason. Now you will never breathe a word of this, will you? You know they would make Masons of us if they knew we told."

"Heavens! they wouldn't dare ——"

"Yes, they would. Now swear to me you will never scold your husband again, for he has suffered enough; and if he lives through this night, he will need your kindest treatment, or he may become a driveling idiot from the shock, as many another man has done."

Mrs. Dillydally threw her arms around her friend's neck and sobbed, "If they spare his life, I will never speak another harsh word to him again, never! I swear it, so '*mote it be!*'"

Because She Loved Him So

Comedy Monologue for a Lady

By Agnes Electra Platt

Because She Loved Him So

CHARACTER.—Mrs. Jack Weldon, a devoted wife.
SCENE.—Sitting-room in the Weldon apartment.
TIME.—8:30 A. M.

Enter MRS. W.—*paces floor while talking.*

Oh, I do believe I shall go stark, staring mad within the next ten minutes if Jack doesn't come. I sat up till two o'clock last night, or rather this morning, thinking every minute he would be here, and then when I finally *did* go to bed I didn't shut my eyes all night long. I was a perfect wreck this morning when I woke up. I think it would melt Jack's heart if he could see what suffering he has caused. But, of course, he is not to blame—he is dead or he would have sent me some word. He has been kept late at the office once or twice before; but last night he didn't come home at all. (*Throws herself in chair and weeps.*)

I got so nervous by nine o'clock I just couldn't stand it, and so I called up police headquarters and gave them a complete description of him. I pretended I'd seen a man like that lurking around here, and thought he might be a burglar. I knew *that* would set them hunting—whereas if I simply told them I'd lost my husband, they'd only laugh—like that hateful Mrs. Swift down-stairs, who said: "You'll find after a while, my dear, that you have more peace of mind when you *don't* know where your husband is than when you do."

Spiteful thing, I can't bear her. I like cats for animals, but I do dislike people of that variety. (*Gets up and paces floor again*).

Oh, this is awful; this horrible suspense is simply killing me, and the worst of it is I don't even dare call up his office to know when he left there last night! He was furious with me once before when I got nervous because he wasn't home at the usual time and called them up. He said he was a laugh-

23

ing stock for days; it looked as though he had a wife who couldn't trust him; but mercy! the way the men act nowadays, why shouldn't wives be on their guard?—but of course Jack is not one of that kind, and he told me the next time I didn't know where he was, not to advertise it at his place of business and entertain the clerks with my anxieties. But now that I come to think of it he's been late a good deal lately. You don't suppose —— Oh, no—it can't be—I won't even think such a thing of Jack. Oh, dear, I've been to that 'phone at least fifty times! It seems the most natural thing in the world to *do* something. ·If a wife loves her husband, why *shouldn't* she be anxious when he's been gone since yesterday morning? And why should a man be ashamed to have folks know that his wife loves him? But he'd be furious with me—even if he were dead,—if I should let them know he didn't come home last night. Perhaps he's been planning this all along, and has eloped with his stenographer or something. Now, I come to think of it, that's just what he *has* done. Why haven't I thought of it before? I remember his praising her once—said " She was good-natured and painstaking ——'' Well, what else is there for homely folks to do but be good-natured; they can't afford to be anything else, and she *is* homely. I saw to that myself, when he engaged her. My! but she would fade a carpet. Oh, of course she was good-natured to him. Now I see it all; she has just been scheming for this all the time, while I, his poor, unsuspecting, little wife —— (*Collapses on sofa in tears, suddenly jumps up and wipes eyes.*) What a fool I am to be crying for such a man! I'll just forget there ever was such a person. I'll begin hating him this minute. The brute!—But maybe he isn't a brute—maybe all the while I'm saying these awful things his poor body is floating in the East River or somewhere. (*Speaks to maid at door.*) What is it, Mary? Oh, the morning paper! No—I don't want any breakfast, Mary. No, nothing at all. Oh, I just hate to open this paper for fear it will tell of some unidentified body being found, or I will be confronted by a glaring headline, " Unknown Man Foully Murdered.''

If there *is* such a heading, I'll know it's you, Jack. How could I think for a minute you would desert your own dear wife for that ugly stenographer with her pudgy nose and pudgier clothes. Oh, but if you *have* gone off with her—there *will* be murder, deliberate, premeditated, " in the first degree murder,'' planned out to the smallest detail and executed in the most torturesome manner ! I'll tear her eyes out so she'll never " goo-goo " at another married man.

Now, I'll know the worst. (*Opens paper.*) No, there's nothing except about some actress marrying a millionaire. Well, I hope he won't desert her at the end of two years, as my husband has me. What is this ? " Man run over by trolley." Oh, that's Jack; that's Jack ! I'll sue the company for no end of damages. Now, that's just like Jack—thoughtful of me to the very last. (*Wipes eyes.*) Let's see what it says. Oh, no, it was only a street cleaner ! Well, it serves him right for being in the way. Why didn't he keep on the sidewalk ? I've no patience with such people.

Here's a woman offers big reward for the return of her dog. What foolishness ! But advertising seems to be the way people find lost things. I s'pose I could advertise for Jack—— (*Suddenly.*) Why, of course that's the *thing* to do ! What a fool I've been to waste all this time. I'll call up the—— (*Mentions local paper. Goes to 'phone.*)

Central, give me *The Morning Eagle*, please. What number ? Oh, I don't know their number, but do hurry ! What's that ! You must have the number. Oh, bother ! (*Turns to directory.*) How hateful of her ! Why don't she look it up herself? Well, here it is. (*Turns to 'phone.*) Give me 6784 Melcombe. What? You haven't any such number? Oh, wait a minute, I guess I read it backward. (*Looks again at book.*) Oh, yes, it's 3297—ugh ! It was near enough ! She is just trying to aggravate me, and I'm so confused I can't think straight. Now for pity sake what shall I say ? Oh, 'course I won't let them know who I am ! Hello ! Hello, is this *The Eagle* office ? Well, I want to advertise for my (*hesitatingly*)—that is I want to offer a reward for—for some information about—about a man. Yes. What? What kind of a man? Well you needn't laugh. This is far from being a joke, I can tell you. What's that? Can I describe him? Of course I can. Don't you suppose I can describe my, own—— (*Stops suddenly; aside.*) Oh, goodness ! That was a narrow escape. (*In 'phone.*) Yes, I can describe him perfectly. He's tall—oh, I don't know exactly how tall by feet; but I should say six or seven. That would be tall, wouldn't it? Yes—and he's dark. What's that? Very dark? Why he's not a mulatto. Oh, I don't know how much he weighs; but he is quite big—I think he must weigh a good deal. No—he doesn't wear a moustache, I won't let him. What did he

wear when last seen? (*Aside.*) Oh, these are the same
questions those horrid police people asked me. I do believe
I'm going to cry. (*In 'phone in trembling voice.*) He wore—
I don't quite remember, but I think it was a navy blue tie with
little white specks over it, and a little gold horse-shoe pin I
gave him last Christmas. That all? Why no—he wears eye
glasses and a silk hat—that is on Sundays. His suit? Well,
it was either his gray or his brown one, and he had on patent
leather shoes. What? Where was he last seen? (*Aside.*)
Now, what shall I say? I don't want to say at breakfast yesterday morning. Oh, I know. I did watch him get on a car
in front of the house; he waved me good-bye. (*On 'phone.*)
Hello! He was last seen boarding a down town car in front
of 782 Lincoln Avenue. Is that all? Oh, yes a liberal reward for information of course. Hundreds of dollars. Oh,
do put it on the front page in big type! Yes, and —— Oh,
wait a minute, you'd better put in a Personal! Say—(*very
much affected*), "Dear Jack, if you are alive come back to me
and all will be forgiven, and no questions asked." Oh, sign
it "Broken Heart." Have you got it? Yes, I guess that's all.
(*Turns dramatically from 'phone.*) And now I must wait.
Yes, I will try and wait the coming of some direful messenger
to tell me I'm a deserted wife or a widow. (*Turns to door.*)
What's that, Mary? A policeman to see me? What do you
mean? Well, show him in of course.

(*Stands waiting expectantly.*) Perhaps this tragedy is going
to unfold a little. Ah, good-morning, sir! Yes, I'm Mrs.
Weldon. What? You called in regard to the man I described
as having been seen hanging around here last night. (*Excitedly.*) Oh, yes, have you found him? What! (*Shrieks.*)
You've had him locked up in a cell all night! Found him
boldly trying to enter the front door late last night, and you
want me to come down and identify him. (*Sinks weakly in a
chair.*) Oh, what have I done! What have I done! (*Springs
up.*) Sir, do you know that man is my *husband?* How *dared*
you lock him up? Don't you know I've nearly gone mad
wondering what had become of him, while you had him locked
up in a horrid, stuffy, old cell. What? Yes, of *course* I
asked you to find him, and of *course* I said he was a burglar;
but can't you see it was only to make you *hunt* for him.
Can't you tell a gentleman from a burglar? Oh, Mary, bring
my hat and coat quick! These silly policemen have locked up
my Jack. I might have known nothing but prison bars would

have kept him away. Oh, hurry, Mary! This despicable man says if I want my husband I must come to the jail and get him. (*Pantomime of putting on hat while talking.*) Fancy having to identify your own husband, if I " want him." Oh, but I'll go, for I *do* want him. Oh, what will he say to me for getting him into such a scrape! Well, I don't care what he says, or if he *kills* me. It's some comfort to know where he is at last; and, now, *on to the rescue.* (*To policeman.*) Yes, sir, I'm ready. Is the patrol wagon at the door? I'd like to get to that burglar in a hurry.

(*To audience.*) Well, I've learned a lesson, and now for the moral.

Young wives, when your husband comes late at night, don't call the police in awful fright. In other words, don't play the dunce. Just keep it quiet if he's gone six months. [*Exit.*

Helping Father in a Business Deal

Comedy Monologue for a Lady

By Agnes Electra Platt

HELPING FATHER IN A BUSINESS DEAL.

CHARACTER. — Miss Jeanette Robins.
COSTUME. — Street dress, slightly awry.
SCENE. — Sitting-room.

MISS ROBINS (*enters, carrying small parcels*). It's a funny thing that you can't put on your old clothes to run out and do a little shopping without meeting every swell in town. You can roam all day in your best togs without meeting a soul you care about. (*Glances in mirror.*)

Dear me! my hat is off on one ear and I look as though I'd been circling the Flatiron Building on a windy day; and if I didn't run right into that stuck-up Maud Barrett with a college friend from the West who is visiting her. I could just feel her eyes glued on that glove without the button, and could imagine her hateful comments after I passed along. But she needn't put on so many airs; her dad made his money at shoe-blacking or blacking shoes, I forget which. Anyway, he's one of those self-made men looked down upon by polite society.

(*Opens a parcel containing gloves.*) Now I wonder what possessed me to buy those gloves. I have six pairs now I've never had on, but they were *so* cheap I thought it would be economy. It's very expensive to be economical.

Papa makes so much fun of my purchases! Now those marked down opera-glasses I bought last week — they were such a bargain. I just couldn't resist; but of course it was foolish, as I had no use for them, having two pairs already. But I can give them to Mary for Christmas. Papa said I had better remember the grocer with a silk hat and cane. Papa can be so disagreeable when he takes a notion! I don't see any reason just because people are servants why we should always be reminding them of it by presenting them with calico aprons, etc.

(*Takes off hat and coat.*) Now I must hurry and get my French and music out of the way, for I told Kit I would go to the matinee with her this afternoon.

(*Turns as if addressing someone at door.*) What's that, Mary? For pity's sake, what are you talking about? Is papa crazy? Wants *me* to entertain a gentleman this afternoon till he comes? I don't see how I can; I've an engagement. Oh, dear! I do remember, now, he did say something to me about a man coming here from the West on important business, and must be entertained royally, as it might benefit him pecuniarily, and now he's gone to Philadelphia and won't be back till seven to-night. Isn't that provoking? So inconsiderate of papa! But, then, he isn't to blame for being suddenly called away; but it's rough on me. Imagine my entertaining some old fossil, or perhaps some dreadful cow-boy, till seven o'clock! Well, whatever he is, he no doubt would be better pleased with a pipe and his own society than my clatter; anyhow, I'll have to make the best of it, and call up Kit right away. (*Goes to 'phone.*) 2971 Spring. Hello, is that you, Kit? Well, this is *me*. Say, I can't go this afternoon. No; isn't it abominable? Oh, I've got to stay home and jolly along some stupid old business friend of papa's. You see, he was called out of town unexpectedly, and some one has to be here to give this old bore the glad hand. I wouldn't mind if he was young and handsome, but that's never my luck. I guess his business is something awfully important, for papa never puts himself out for anyone unless it is, and he has been stocking up with cigars and — well, liquid refreshments at a great rate. It can't be helped, but we'll make up for this some other time, and papa shall come down handsomely to pay for our disappointment. Good-by.

Now I'll resign myself to misery. Here's his old telegram. (*Picks up from table.*) "Will probably arrive 3 P. M. Tuesday. — Southwick."

Southwick — what a ridiculous name! Why didn't they make it Lampwick? I'm sure it would be more appropriate for a man who owns a whole oil mine. Why, this old duffer — I s'pose he's old — of course he is — must be furiously rich. He's the one papa speaks of so much. I reckon he keeps poor papa guessing some of the time. It

may be worth while to get him good-natured. I'll just try
it. I wonder if I had better change my dress? If I lay
myself out, I'll bet I can get him so rattled we can wind
him right round our finger, and if papa makes a go of this
deal I'll strike him for that set of furs I've wanted so long.
There's nothing slow about me when I once get started.
Now, Mr. Lampwick, you want to look out; if I don't play
the agreeable to you it will be mighty funny.

Heigh-ho! I'll bet he's coming up the walk now.
(*Goes to window.*) Sure as I'm alive! (*Looks at clock.*)
He's ahead of time — but he won't get ahead of me. Am
I dreaming? Young and good-looking, sure as the world
— a great, stalwart, manly fellow — and here I was looking for a little, wizened up, baldheaded old patriarch.
Dear! I wish I had changed my dress! Gracious! I
can't believe it yet. It's too good to be true. There's
the bell. I'm all in a flutter! Mary has gone to answer it. Heart, be still! Steady, Jeanette, he's coming!
(*Turns to door and extends hand.*) Ah! How do you
do? I shall be obliged to introduce myself. I'm Mr.
Robin's daughter. You are the gentleman, I presume, that
papa was expecting this afternoon on business. He re-
gretted not being able to welcome you, but an imperative
call took him out of town, and I'm to try and entertain
you till he returns. Take this easy chair — do. You
must be quite tired travelling — nothing so wearing, I
think. You arrived in the city to-day, I understand.
Yes? Are you to be with us some time? Depends upon
business? Oh, yes, of course; you men always put business before pleasure, don't you? What? You find business and pleasure combined this afternoon? Oh, how
kind of you to say so! (*Aside.*) He's all right; we're
progressing finely. (*Aloud.*) Oh, no, indeed; you're not
detaining me from anything more pleasurable. I should
really have been quite dull here this afternoon. (*Aside.*)
His eyes are simply gorgeous! I hope papa misses his train.
(*Aloud.*) I'm afraid I shall be very dull company, though,
for business and politics and such subjects which interest men are so entirely out of woman's sphere. Papa says
we girls can't talk about anything but parties and dress.
What's that? You're interested in such things? Oh,

that's nice of you to say so! I always thought men must like such things, or we shouldn't be so dreadfully fond of them ourselves. You dance, of course. Yes; I'm passionately fond of it, but have had to give it up lately. Was stupid enough to sprain my ankle last summer at a house party. Yes; it was dreadfully provoking. The very first day I was there, too. They made me stay, and were all so attentive — the men especially — they tried to make me think they enjoyed waiting on me. What nonsense! How absurd! I'm sure they felt like martyrs. Excuse me. What is it, Mary? A gentleman to see Mr. Robins? Well, tell him he's out of town. What's that? Said he must see some of the family? What cheek! Some book agent, I presume. Tell him Mr. Robins is out of town for a month and Miss Robins is engaged. I guess that will settle him. How annoying these agents are, and we are simply besieged! What's that? You feel honored that you didn't meet with the same fate. As though I couldn't tell an agent when I see one! Oh, no, indeed; papa is very anxious to see you and will soon be here, and I hope your business may be arranged satisfactorily. (*Aside.*) I guess I won't tell him about the furs. (*Aloud.*) I sincerely hope this delay in seeing him will not greatly inconvenience you. (*Looking at window.*)

Well, Mary must have had quite a time getting rid of that agent. He's just going down the walk, gesticulating at a great rate. Why, he acts perfectly furious! He must be crazy. I wonder if he thinks we're obliged to receive every man that comes here selling patent flour sifters and the like. We ought to keep a dog. I think dogs are perfectly fascinating, don't you? What? You often become unpleasantly attached to them in your business? Really, how funny you are! I know you get on beautifully with dogs. They say, you know, that children and dogs are the best diviners of character. (*Turns to door.*)

What is it, Mary? That man left his card with a message. Let me see. Probably some crank. "Lemuel R. Southwick, Pres. of Birmington Oil Co." Why, what does this mean? (*Sternly.*) Who are you, sir? Isn't your name Southwick? No? Harold Jones, representing the

Acme Book Co.! Heavens! what have I done? Sent away the man papa was so anxious to meet and been entertaining a *book agent !* This accounts for the rage he was in.

(*Reads.*) "Had reached a conclusion favorable to you in the matter under consideration, but the treatment I have received at your house compels me to resume my first decision. Do not approach me on this matter again."

Oh, how awful! How will I ever meet papa! You, Mr. Brown — Smith — Jones, or whatever you call yourself, take yourself out of sight and hearing, and be thankful we've no dog. Go! You knew there was a mistake. Do you think I would have wasted my time on a miserable book agent? (*Pointing to door.*) Go, I say! (*Sinks into chair.*)

What a fool I've been! Lost my head completely over a cheap travelling agent simply because he had handsome eyes! What a mess! I wonder how it will affect papa financially. I can stand his anger, but I do hate to give up *that set of furs.*

CURTAIN.

Through the Keyhole

A Monologue for a Lady

By Arthur L. Tubbs

Through the Keyhole

SCENE.—*Handsomely furnished private parlor in a first-class hotel. Door in* F., *with lock and key; door* R. *leads to sleeping apartment. At* L. *is a large screen, which hides a door leading to another room. This door is locked and there is no key. Down* R. C. *a table, on which are a few books and one or two newspapers. An easy chair* L. *of table. Across corner, up* R. *or* L., *is a sofa. Desk, with writing materials, down* L. *Other belongings and ornaments of a rather luxurious apartment.*

(After curtain rises, ANGELINA *enters door in* F., *in frantic haste, greatly agitated, dropping several bundles on the floor. Her large hat is pushed down over her eyes, her skirt is torn from the band at the back, and she presents a generally upset and flustered appearance. As soon as she enters, she slams the door shut and starts to lock it, but, finding no key, turns and leans against door, panting for breath.)*

ANGELINA. Oh, dear! Oh, goodness! Was ever—was *ever* a woman so frightened as I am? Did a woman *ever* have such a narrow escape? Narrow? I should say so—so narrow that I'm not even sure I have had it. *(Looking distractedly about.)* If I could only find that key! *(Bends over, searching about floor, then suddenly springs up and again puts her back to the door.)* I thought I heard him! He's coming! What shall I do? I dare not scream; if I do, he'll rush in and murder me before anybody else gets here. *(She is all the time peering about for the key, and now sees it on the floor, just out of her reach.)* Oh, there it is! *(She now has an awkward time trying to reach the key without leaving the door.)* Oh! oh! I can't reach it! *(Reaches out with her foot, holds the door with one hand and reaches with the other, etc., but*

3

fails to get the key ; all the time talking.)   To think of a married woman running away from her own husband like this.
Husband, yes; but such a fearfully, dreadfully, perfectly awful
jealous husband !   Oh, if I only *could* reach it !   I know he
wants to kill me—I'm sure of it !   Ever since I began proceed-
ings for a divorce, I have felt that he intends to kill me.   He
thinks I want a divorce so as to marry Jack Halstead.   The
idea ! (*She has removed her hat and is about to toss it to
one side, when she is struck by a bright idea : by using the hat
she is able to reach the key and draws it to her.*)   Saved !
Saved at last !   Kind heaven, I thank thee ! (*She attempts to
lock the door, but in her agitation cannot find the keyhole.*)
Oh, where *is* that keyhole ?   I'm not drunk, but I can't find
the keyhole.   It's gone ; there isn't any !   Oh, yes, there is !
There ! (*She succeeds in locking the door.*)   Thank goodness !
(*Comes down and sinks into a chair, taking her hat and fan-
ning herself with it.*)   I've escaped with my life.   But for how
long ?   I saw Tom following me.   He will keep it up until he
catches me, and then—then—but it is my fate, I feel it.
(*Pausing, then in a collected manner.*)   But, dear me, if he's
coming, I don't want him to find me looking like this. (*She
rises and examines herself.*)   Somebody stepped on my dress
and tore it half off. (*She is pinning it on.*)   How my hair
looks !   Well, I can't help it—I just *had* to sue Tom for a
divorce, for he was paying that Sallie Dickson altogether too
much attention.   And then, he was so foolish.   Why, he got
jealous without any cause ; thought I cared for Jack Halstead.
(*Picks up packages, etc.*)   How silly !   What if Jack *did* happen to call once or twice when Tom was out, and what if we
did happen to meet on the street a few times and walk along
together ?   That wasn't any harm.   If Tom hadn't been so—
and I—why, I know that letter to him in a woman's hand
writing was from Sallie Dickson, and—well, when he threat-
ened to get a divorce, that time, I just made up my mind I'd get
ahead of him and get my application in first ; and I did.   How
furious he was !   I know he intends to kill me ! (*Coolly.*)
Well, anyway, if he does, I want to look my best when it happens.   Let—me—see : my pink ?   No, that white lace over
pale blue, with the chiffon ruffles.   But I don't know as that's
so becoming as my amber satin, after all.   I wonder which would
match the blood best, if he should cut my throat ?   But if he
should *shoot* me, there might not be any blood to speak of.   I
do hope he will leave me spread out gracefully when all the

people rush in. Ugh! It's kind of horrible when you come to think of it. Poor Tom, I didn't think he would ever become a murderer. His own wife, too. Now,—(*There is suddenly a sharp rapping on the door in flat. She starts violently and stands trembling, with terror-stricken face. The knocking is repeated.*) Oo-o-o! O-oh! 'Tis he! My time is come! And I haven't had a chance to change my dress yet. This looking thing! (*The knocking again. She calls, timidly, in a piping little voice.*) W-e-l-l?

Boy's Voice (*without*). Mrs. Witherby in?

Ang. (*to herself*). Shall I answer? No, I won't. It may be ——

Voice (*louder*). Is that Mrs. Witherby?

Ang. I'll risk it. But no,—no! It might be Tom, disguising his voice. It is! Still, it doesn't sound a bit like Tom's voice.

Voice. Mrs. Witherby, are you *in*?

Ang. N-no,—I mean—(*aside*) it *isn't* Tom's voice 'I'm sure of it. (*Aloud.*) I—(*aside*) but it may be his hired assassin,—he may be there, too. Ah, ha! no, sir! I'm not to be caught so easily.

Voice (*very loudly*). Here's a package for Mrs. Witherby!

Ang. Oh, a package! Very well. (*About to unlock door.*) Er—a—just leave it there by the door, please. I'm not dressed. (*Aside.*) What a fib! Well, I mean not dressed *up*.

Voice. Can't. You got to sign this receipt.

Ang. Receipt? Oh, dear! Well—a—(*cautiously*)—why, just slip it under the door, please. (*A piece of folded yellow paper comes through under the door. She picks it up and is about to open it, when she pauses, suspiciously.*) No! It may contain a poisoned powder which will fly out and kill me instantly. My wits do not desert me. I'll open it, though,—so! (*She gets a newspaper from the table, at the same time getting a handkerchief, which she holds over her nose. She then holds the yellow paper at arm's length over the newspaper and lets it open, shaking it. The newspaper is on the floor and she quickly folds it over with her foot and stands upon it, meanwhile holding the yellow piece of paper behind her and shaking it vigorously, still with the handkerchief over her nose. Finally she looks at the receipt.*) "One box." I wonder if it means a box at the theatre, or a box of what? (*Goes to desk, takes pen and is about to sign.*) Maybe it is Tom's decree of divorce in disguise, and he takes this way of getting me to sign it.

(*Looks at it closely.*) But no, there are no names except my own; it must be all right. (*She signs it.*) There! (*Goes and tucks the paper under the door.*) There it is. Now go away. (*Waits an instant.*) Are you gone? (*Listens.*) You gone? (*Puts her ear to keyhole.*) I don't hear them breathing. I wonder what's in that box. (*She unlocks the door cautiously, opens it a mere crack, then quickly slams it shut again and locks it. Gets down, removing the key, and looks through the keyhole.*) I don't see anybody. They must be gone. (*Opens the door, reaches out and takes in a good-sized white pasteboard box, hastily closing and again locking the door. Takes the box to table, curiously looking at the inscription upon it.*) "To Mrs. Thomas K. Witherby." Now, whose writing is that? I don't know it. Perhaps—yes, it may be Tom's disguised, and it—it may contain an infernal machine that will blow me to atoms the moment I open it! (*There is a large rubber band around the box; she absent-mindedly lifts it up and lets it snap against the box, which it does with a sharp noise. She springs back, affrighted, with a scream, and tumbles over upon the floor, where she lies for a moment motionless, then partly rises very cautiously and looks about.*) Did it go off? Am I all here? (*Feels of her head, her arms, etc., as she slowly sits up.*) I seem to be all right. Why, it didn't go off at all. I wonder—— (*Rises and looks at the box.*) Oh, it was only that rubber band. (*Snaps it again.*) That's what it was. But I'm so nervous. (*Lifts the box carefully.*) It's too light to be an infernal machine. I'll open it. (*She opens the box, with some misgivings, and takes out a beautiful bunch of roses, to which is tied a card.*) From Jack Halstead. Oh, I ought not to keep them;—but I will! They're just too sweet! Yes, I'll wear them to-night—why, yes, this is the night of Mrs. Farrington's entertainment and I have promised to recite a piece. I wonder if all this excitement has driven it out of my head. I'll just try it over. Anyhow, if Tom is determined to end my existence, I'll try and elude him for one more good time, to-night. Let me see, how does that piece go? Oh, yes; I remember. (*She reads a selection ad libitum.*) There, now that's all right, I think I'll change my dress. I'll wear—yes, my very best. It may be my last appearance in public, and I want to leave a good impression. (*Exit* R. *and returns at once with an elegant evening gown, which she holds up and admires. Is about beginning to disrobe, when she pauses suddenly, sniffing.*) Seems to me I smell cigar smoke. (*She sniffs again.*) I do. It smells like a good cigar, too. Now, where can it come from? Smells just like the kind Tom used to smoke. (*As she is looking about, there comes the sound of the whistling of a gay tune in the room off* L. *She pauses and listens.*) Whistling! It must be a *man!* (*Looking towards* L.) In there! (*Goes and looks behind screen.*) Why, yes, there's a door there, and I never knew it. It must lead to another sleeping-room just like mine on that side. (*She listens; the whistling continues. It is the tune of a popular love song.*) Why, where have I heard that tune before? It sounds so familiar. It makes me think of something—of somebody—of *Tom!* Yes, it is that song he always liked so well. (*The whistling stops and a strong masculine voice is heard singing the words of the same song. She starts in surprise, and listens with suppressed emotion.*) Tom! It's Tom's voice! And—oh, what if he means to kill me! He does! He will! Help! Help! Murder! Help! (*She is greatly alarmed, wringing her hands in dismay. The singing ceases. She runs to door in* F. *and is about to exit, then pauses.*) No, I dare not go out there; he might meet me in the hall. There is no escape! I—I must meet my fate. But I'll die like a man—I mean like a woman!

MAN'S VOICE. (*off* L.). What is it? Is anything the matter?

(*She pulls the screen aside and sees that there is no key in the door.*)

ANG. The key is on the other side. I am at his mercy!

VOICE. Who's in there? Is that you, Angelina?

ANG. He knows me. I am lost!

VOICE. Angelina, are you in there?

ANG. No; it isn't I! It's—— Oh, yes it is, Tom. Oh, Tom, spare me! Have mercy, Tom, *dear* Tom! It was all a mistake. I don't love Jack Halstead. It's you I love, Tom—you! Spare my life! (*She is kneeling by the door, as if pleading at his feet.*)

VOICE. What do you mean, Angelina? What's the matter?

ANG. (*aside*). He pretends not to know.

VOICE. Put your ear to the keyhole.

ANG. (*about to do as he requests, then quickly getting away; aside*). He wants to shoot me through the keyhole!

(*Aloud.*)   Oh, Tom, would you murder me?   I am innocent. Have mercy!

Voice.   Nonsense! I want to tell you something.

(*She listens, as he is evidently saying something too low for the audience to hear; gradually she gets her ear to the key-hole and listens for a moment, while a smile dawns upon her face and she looks very happy.*)

Ang.   Then you were running after me only to tell me how sorry you were and to ask my forgiveness for being jealous? And you don't blame me at all, and—oh, Tom, do you mean it?   Of course I forgive you, you silly fellow.   Eh?   No, there's no key on this side, either.   Can't you open it?   Neither can I.   What?   Blow a kiss through the keyhole?   How ridiculous! Oh, Tom—say! I want you to take me to Mrs. Carrington's reception to-night.   Will you?   What?   Why, of course. Come around to the hall door and I'll give you twenty—as many as you want.   And—oh, Tom!   Which dress shall I wear?   The white over blue?   All right.   That's the one I— oh, very well!   (*She jumps up and goes to door* F.; *is about to unlock it when she remembers something, goes to table, hastily gathers up the roses, box, paper, etc.   As she is doing so, the door* F. *is tried from without.   She quickly tosses the roses, etc., over behind the sofa, out of sight, and goes to the door and unlocks it.   Just as she opens the door, she exclaims.*)   Oh, Tom!   (*As she is supposed to fall into his arms, the curtain falls.*)

The Proposal

A Monologue for a Gentleman

By Hector Fezandie

THE PROPOSAL.

SCENE. — EDWARD STEWART'S *room in a New York boarding-house of the present time.*

STEWART (*outside*). Called to see me? A lady? (*Enters.*) Who the deuce could it have been? (*Holds the door ajar as if speaking to some one outside.*) What! Left an umbrella for me, and said I would understand? (*Closes the door.*) An umbrella! Can it be? . . . It is! My umbrella that I bought yesterday morning and lost yesterday afternoon! It was a good idea of mine to have my name and address engraved on the handle. I'm blessed if I ever expected to see the umbrella again, though, after that stout man walked off with it. It's bad enough to be absent-minded, and it's worse to have a conscience; but when these two evils combine in a single individual — well, that single individual is apt at times to find life a burden. Now, that's just my case. My absent-mindedness is something phenomenal; it is forever getting me into all manner of scrapes. On the other hand, my conscience is abnormal; it is a morbid growth. I am ashamed of it, but I can't help it. And that's how I came to lose my umbrella. I boarded an elevated train yesterday afternoon with my brand-new umbrella in my hand, found a seat, for a wonder — or as much of a seat as the stout man next to me did not overflow into, and was soon — well — in fact, I was wondering whether if I were to ask Lucy to be mine, there would be any chance — or rather I was revolving in my mind how I should say it, and what she would reply, and what would happen then, and — sweet Lucy, how I do love that girl! But that's not what I started out to say. Let me see, where was I? Oh, yes. All of a sudden I started up with the impression that I had passed my station; but I hadn't, we were only at Twenty-third Street and I was going to One Hundred and Twenty-fifth. As I rose, I saw an umbrella fall. My stout neighbor had just stepped off the car, and the gateman had pulled the bell-rope. It flashed upon me that my fat friend was forgetting his umbrella. Without a moment's hesitation, I picked it up, rushed out upon the platform of the now moving car, and throwing the umbrella out as far as I could, I shouted at the top of my voice: "Hey, there; you've forgotten your umbrella!" The obese individual turned around at the sound of my voice and looked puzzled; but, before

3

I lost sight of him I had the satisfaction of seeing one of the station employees hand him the umbrella. Then I went back to my seat with an easy conscience, to discover that I had forced my own brand-new umbrella upon the unsuspecting stout gentleman. That's what comes of having an abnormal conscience! Of course I stopped at the next station and took the train back to Twenty-third Street, and of course I didn't find the slightest trace of the umbrella or the least clew to the identity of the fat man. But what I should like to know is how that identical umbrella now finds its way back to me, and from the hands of a lady too. Perhaps "Mrs. Stout Gentleman" is afflicted with a conscience too, which prevents her from keeping the umbrellas purloined by her husband. (*Opens the umbrella. A letter and a newspaper fall out.*)

Hello, what's this! A letter — and a newspaper. (*Examining the letter.*) It's addressed to me. Queer way of sending a letter, done up in an umbrella. Looks like a woman's writing. (*Reading.*) "My dear, *dear* friend." Her dear, *dear* friend. That's a curious way for a woman to address a man she's never met. "My dear, dear friend, I trust it will not seem unwomanly in me to style you thus, for although our acquaintance has been of short duration as measured by the arbitrary standards of men, the thrilling circumstances under which we met surely give me the privilege of thus addressing one who has earned my everlasting gratitude." What the deuce does the woman mean? "I had hoped to see you this morning and to convey to you in my own name, as well as in that of my six little fatherless angels, the heartfelt thanks which emotion prevented me from adequately expressing last night. Owing to my intense excitement at the time, I am ashamed to say that your very features are unknown to me. I saw you as in a dream. But I hope soon to have the privilege of renewing an acquaintance — may I say a friendship — which on my part, at least, shall continue until my dying day. Very, very sincerely your friend, Julia Simpkins.

"P. S. I return your umbrella. From it I found your name and address."

By Jove, that's a remarkable document; "thrilling circumstances under which we met — everlasting gratitude — six little fatherless angels " — my fair correspondent appears to be a widow " — emotion — intense excitement — a friendship which, on my part at least, shall continue until my dying day." I suppose my stout friend generously loaned my umbrella to this interesting widow during the shower yesterday afternoon. But who would have supposed him capable of inspiring such tender, I may say such fervid, sentiments in the heart of a fair stranger, and by such commonplace methods, too? True, the sentimental widow admits she did not see the features of this Don Juan *au parapluie.* (*Picks up the envelope.*) Hello, here's a second postscript on the envelope which I had not seen. (*Reading.*) "See marked article in the enclosed copy of the *Herald.*" Marked article, eh? (*Opening the paper.*) Here it is. (*Reading.*) "A Modest Hero."

What's this ? (*Reads again.*) " As the ferry-boat was leaving the slip a beautiful young woman rushed down the gangway. In her excitement she did not notice that the boat had already started, nor did she see a gentleman who stood on the end of the bridge waving a farewell with his umbrella to some friend on the boat. When Mrs. Julia Simpkins took in the situation it was already too late. She was unable to come to a sudden stop on the slippery incline, and ran full tilt into the gentleman, who was unaware of her presence. The force of the collision caused him to lose his balance, and in an instant, to the horror of the spectators, both were lost to sight beneath the icy waters of the East River. Presently they rose to the surface. Mrs. Simpkins, with admirable presence of mind, had thrown her arms about the gentleman's neck, and was clinging to him with the energy of despair, while he struggled heroically with the buffeting waves, and endeavored to scale the slippery piles. When at length the couple were saved from their perilous position the lady's arms were still twined about her brave rescuer's neck, and she sobbed hysterically upon his manly breast. This touching scene drew many a sympathetic tear from the eyes of the spectators." How romantic. " But the blushing hero of this adventure, with the modesty which is always characteristic of true courage, slipped off unobserved and without even leaving his name. He had, however, forgotten his umbrella, on which was found the name Edward Stewart, 5061 Lexington Avenue."

My umbrella, by Jove ! The alleged hero must have been my stout friend of the elevated train. Ha ! ha ! he must have floated like a cork. I can imagine him floundering in the water with a buxom widow clinging to his neck, while he struggled to free himself, and spluttered, half choked with salt water and fear. Ha ! ha ! Those reporters are comical fellows. But I wish they could have left my name out of this ridiculous affair. Well, let's see the end of it. (*Reading.*) "Who knows but that this adventure may prove only the beginning of a charming romance? All honor and happiness to the modest hero, Edward Stewart !" Yes, it says distinctly "the modest hero, Edward Stewart." I see how it was. Of course, they thought the umbrella belonged to the stout party. Modest hero ! How well that looks in print. (*Glancing over the paper.*) When you come to read it attentively that is really a very well-written account. I can see just how it happened. A gentleman is waving a farewell — perhaps to his sweetheart, who is on the ferry-boat — just as I might have been doing to Lucy. Suddenly, without a moment's warning, he finds himself in the river. A human being is beside him. Calm, in the midst of danger, forgetting himself for his fellow-being, feeling the anxious and admiring gaze of his distracted sweetheart upon him (*excitedly, forgetting himself*), I grasped the sinking form of the young woman in one hand, and amid the deafening applause of the crowd I bore her safely to the shore. Then, exhausted and dripping with the icy waters of the East River, I reached Lucy's side just in time to catch her faint‑ing form. When, with slowly returning consciousness, her beautiful eyes met mine, they yielded the thrilling though unspoken message of requited love! How beautiful! How inspiring! How little we realize the latent sublimity of human character until occasion brings it to the light!

I wonder if Lucy has read the paper to-day. (*Looking at the paper.*) "A Modest Hero!" I shouldn't be at all surprised if she has, for I have heard her say that she made it a point to read the news every day. Perhaps she is reading it at this very minute! I hope she will not feel jealous of the charming widow. I don't know, though; perhaps a little wholesome jealousy would be favorable to my prospects. I have always heard and read that a woman never really appreciates her suitor's qualities until some other woman has discovered them. Of course my conduct shall be irreproachable in this matter, but I don't care if she feels just a trifle — just the least bit — jealous. If she does, she will be able to realize how I feel when I see her with that puppy, J. Montague Smythe, confound him! I wonder if it wouldn't be a good time now to send her that proposal which I spent three nights in com‑posing, and which I have carried in my pocket ever since, because I have not dared to send it? (*Takes paper from his pocket.*) Let me see. This is the one in blank verse, this is the sonnet, ah! here it is. (*Examining the document.*) Yes, that is really quite good, and I shall never have a better chance than the present to send it.

I must make a clean copy of it, though, for the date on this one has grown old since it was written. (*Seats himself at table and writes.*) It's curious how sanguine I feel about this to-day. I was never able to get my courage to the sticking-point before; but I have often heard that the men who are bravest in the face of danger are the most arrant cowards in the presence of the woman they love. I suppose there is a good deal of truth in that. There now, there's my last card. If this does not win the game, nothing will. But I am hopeful; I feel that my star is in the ascendant to-day. Now, then, to send the question whose answer will decide my fate. Oh, by the way, I suppose I shall have to make some sort of a reply to the fair widow. (*Conceitedly.*) And I may as well cut short this sentimental business at the start. Let me see. (*Writing.*) "Mrs. Julia Simpkins . . . Dear Madam . . . I have to acknowledge the receipt of your kind favor of this date . . . together with my umbrella . . . which I regret you should have had . . . the trouble of attending to (*repeating*) of attending to. . . . That's formal enough, I should think, as a starter. . . . (*Writing.*) I am not aware of having done anything to merit the complimentary things you are pleased to write; but, if I have been of service to a fellow-being in any way (*hesitating*) in any way . . . the fact that he is a lady . . . no, that won't do — (*writing*) that fact is of itself sufficient reward. ʼost respectfully yours, Edward Stewart."

There. Now for the address. (*Addresses two envelopes.*) "Miss Lucy Vanderveer, 5073 Lexington Avenue;" "Mrs. Julia Simpkins." (*Seals the letters and rings bell, then goes to the door, which he opens.*) Mary (*to some one outside*), I wish you would have these two letters despatched at once. This one is for Miss Vanderveer at No. 5073, three doors from the corner. You might take that yourself. The other you can send by a district messenger. (*Closes door.*) Well, the deed is done! The die is cast! And now all that remains for me to do is to await the word that shall decide my fate. It will take Mary, say, three minutes to reach the Vanderveers', then say it takes five minutes more before the letter reaches Lucy's hands. Allow fifteen minutes for Lucy to read and answer the letter. In less than half an hour I shall probably know — Ah, darling, if you do but consent! If? Why do I say "*if*"? She will, she must, she shall be mine! Heavens! What if she should refuse me? I was perhaps too impatient. I should have waited a month or two longer. I should have spoken to her myself instead of trusting my fate to ink and paper. My eyes would have been eloquent, even if my tongue had failed me. My emotion would have touched her, while the cold written words will leave her unmoved. Yes, I have made a mistake. (*Rushes for the door.*) Mary! Mary! She's gone! Perhaps I can catch her! (*Takes his hat and rushes out, returning after an instant with a letter in his hand.*)

Too late! Just as I reached the front door, I ran into the servant who was bringing me back the answer. (*Sadly.*) An answer so soon! It must be "no." She would not have replied so promptly if it had been "yes." (*Turning the letter over in his hands.*) I don't dare to open it. Still, the word is written now; it will avail me nothing to defer the blow. (*Opens the letter.*) Eh! What! (*Reading.*) "There is evidently some mistake here. If you have nothing particular to do, drop in for a few minutes. I shall be at home all the afternoon." Some mistake! Hello, why's she written this on the back of my letter! (*Turning letter over.*) By Jove! I've sent her the wrong letter. Ha! ha! ha! I don't wonder she couldn't understand it. Well, so much the better. I'll go this afternoon, I'll go at once, and I'll tell her that I love her, that I adore her, and that she must be mine. For once my absent-mindedness has served me a good turn. (*Puts on his hat and starts to go out. Suddenly recollecting.*) Heavens! If I sent Miss Vanderveer the letter I intended for Mrs. Simpkins, then I must have sent Mrs. Simpkins the letter I meant for Miss Vanderveer. Good gracious, I am lost! I have proposed to the widow! Oh, pshaw, she will see of course that it is a mistake.

Will she, though? Here's the rough draft. Let me see. (*Reads.*) "I can no longer refrain from writing the words which I longed to but dared not utter yesterday before parting from you. I love you! I loved you from the first moment that my eyes rested on your beauty and grace; and in the comparatively short time which has ensued, I have learned to appreciate and admire those qualities of mind and heart which place you so far above any woman I have ever known. I do not presume to imagine that I have already won your affection in return, but if there is the slightest ray of hope, pray give me the benefit of the doubt, until I can strive to gain, and, if possible, to deserve, the prize for which I would gladly lay down my life." (*Despairingly.*) Of course the widow will take all that to herself. There is nothing there to indicate that it was not intended for her. Why, fool that I was, I have not even addressed Lucy by name. I am lost! lost! lost! (*Falls back overcome into a chair. Then suddenly brightening up.*) Perhaps she'll refuse me. Heavens, if she only would! But no, I shall have no such luck as that. She'll accept me. I may as well make up my mind to that. The only question now is, what shall I do *then?* Marry her? It makes my blood run cold when I think of six little orphans calling me papa; six little angels to trot around at night, to cherish, and provide for, and . . . and spank. I might as well marry an orphan asylum at once, and be done with it. But then, on the other hand, if I refuse to marry her I shall be ruined just the same, for like as not I shall land into the horrible notoriety of a breach-of-promise suit! On the strength of that letter any intelligent jury will convict me without leaving their seats. And in either case I am sure to lose Lucy. I can't survive the disgrace! Well, death is easy when there is nothing to live for! (*A knock is heard.*) A knock! It is my knell! It announces the message of death! (*Struggling to be firm.*) Come in! Come in, I say! (*Goes to the door.*) A district messenger with the widow's acceptance! (*As if to some one outside.*) What? Couldn't find the address? Brought back the letter? Oh, my dear, dear boy, you have saved my life! I double your salary! I adopt you! I make you heir to all I — to all I owe! Here; here's a dollar for you, and — and tell your mother to embrace you for me! (*Returning from door, capering and dancing wildly about the room.*) Saved! Saved from the orphan asylum! I live again! I am resurrected, and I shall marry Lucy Vanderveer! I'll go to her at once! I'll fly on the wings of love! (*Picks up his coat, hat and umbrella, and exit hastily.*)

CURTAIN.

Selected Scenes

CONTENTS.

3

FALLEN IN LOVE.

By Rhoda Broughton.

(Adapted.)

CHARACTERS.

JEMIMA, *a cynical old maid.*
LENORE, *her sentimental sister.*

JEMIMA (*entering yawning*). Half-past eight, and Paul and Lenore not returned yet. I will go up-stairs. It certainly would be as well to sleep comfortably and peacefully in bed, as uncomfortably and spasmodically on this hard-bottomed chair; but then, there's all the trouble of getting there. (*Sits down.*) I wonder what a girl like Lenore can see in a man like Paul Le Mesurier. He is ugly, ill-tempered, dissipated; but I suppose when a girl falls in love she thinks — I suppose she thinks — well I am sure I do not care what she thinks.

LENORE (*running in*). Jemima! Jemima! (*Shaking her.*) Wake up, you foolish old person! Are you awake? Wide? Can you understand things?

JEM. It is not your fault if I cannot.

LEN. Stop blinking, and look at me. Do you know that you are looking at the happiest woman in all America?

JEM. And you at the sleepiest.

LEN. (*sitting on arm of her chair*). Don't go to sleep, dear; you don't know what interesting things I have to tell you. Do you know — I dare say you'll hardly believe it at first — I can scarcely believe it myself yet, but — Paul likes me — very — very much.

5

JEM. (*crossly*). Much? There's nothing very wonderful in that. For the last three weeks you have been trying your best to make him like you, and your efforts in that line are not usually unblessed with success.

LEN. (*moving off*). Doing my very best! That's what I was afraid of! So I have — so I have.

JEM. Your friend Paul had no need to see farther through a stone wall than most people, in order to perceive that it was a case of "Whistle, and I'll come to you, my lad!"

LEN. (*excitedly*). Did I do anything to make a person *despise* me, do you think? Was I unladylike? Did I run after him?

JEM. Run after him! Pooh! Nonsense! Paul — Paul! It is an ugly, abrupt little name. Paul Pry! Paul Ferroll, who killed his wife! Are there any more Pauls? You really must have him rechristened, Lenore.

LEN. (*sitting down*). Paul and Virginia. I do not think I am very much like Virginia, though.

JEM. No. And do you mean seriously to tell me that it was with the deliberate intention of asking you to share his exceedingly indifferent fortunes that he took you out on this expedition, in that little dusty, tumble-down, pony-gig in the roasting sun?

LEN. I do not know whether it was deliberate intention or accident, — I rather think it was accident, — but whichever it was, he *did* ask me.

JEM. And you said, "Yes; and thank you kindly," I suppose.

LEN. If I did not say it, I felt it.

JEM. You will at least have an excellent foil on all occasions ready at hand.

LEN. What do you mean? Oh, I see! you think him so ugly?

JEM. Extremely.

LEN. So do I; I like ugliness.

JEM. "Come sit thee down upon this flowery bed,
    While I thy amiable cheeks do coy;
And stick musk roses in thy sleek, smooth head,
    And kiss thy large, fair ears, my gentle joy."

LEN. You are very rude, Jemima, and not at all witty.

JEM. He is poor, too, — unjustifiably poor. I suppose he goes upon the principle that what is not enough for one is enough for two.

LEN. I suppose he does — I like poverty.

JEM. He is ill-tempered. Ah! you remember what a fury he flew into when the boy did not understand him.

LEN. I remember — I like ill-temper.

JEM. He is also a gourmand. Did you notice how thoroughly put out he looked yesterday at dinner because the dessert was gone before it reached him?

LEN. Did he? I dare say — I like greediness. Try as hard as you will, Jemima, you cannot put me out of conceit with him.

JEM. The point I am trying to arrive at is, what could have put you *into* conceit with him? Do not look so angry, my dear child! I am not so wedded to my own opinion but that I am quite ready to change it, if you show me good reason why I should. But — I really do not mean it offensively — but what good qualities of mind or body has Mr. Le Mesurier?

LEN. (*gets up*). How you talk! Do you think that when a person falls in love, they pick out this quality and that, and say, "This is lovable," and "That is lovable," and therefore I will be fond of the person who owns them all? One loves because one loves — because one cannot help it, and because one would not if one could.

JEM. (*gets up*). It isn't so bad your talking that way, but you seem bound to follow it up in actions. I knew a girl at school, a pretty little cat, with eyes as large as saucers, and she used to talk about "mutual affinity" and "falling in love;" but when she came to marry, — why, my dear, he was as old as everybody's grandfather! He was as bald as my hand, as fat as Falstaff, as ignorant as a carp; but he was rich! He made his money from that yellow grease that they put on car wheels.

LEN. How dreadful! Is he alive yet?

JEM. That is what I am coming to. In common justice, he ought to have had creeping paralysis — anything that would have kept her tied to the legs of his bath-chair for the next twenty or thirty years, as a judgment on her for marrying him; instead of which what happens? Why, within four years he is carried off by an attack of apoplexy! Bah! what luck some people have!

LEN. So that is your idea of luck! To marry a commercial ignoramus, and survive him?

JEM. Please remember that I have never been in love.

LEN. Is it possible, Jemima, that in all the many years you have been about the world, you have never had a lover that you cared about with all your heart and soul, for no particularly good reason that you could give yourself or anybody else?

JEM. Never. Humiliating as the confession is, I should have thought, Lenore, that you might have known that I never had a lover, either that I cared about, or that I did not care about. I do not think there are many women of thirty that can make that proud boast. (*Sits down.*)

LEN. Poor Jemima!

JEM. Do not pity me! Appetite comes with eating. If I had *one* lover, I might wish for more; but as the case stands, the more I look around me, the more inclined I am to think that "ignorance is bliss."

LEN. Had any one ever better cause to be happy than I? I am nineteen; I am pretty; I am engaged to the dearest fellow in all the world, who is extremely pleased with me.

JEM.   Instinct tells me you will be miserable together.

LEM.   Poor Jemima!   It is no wonder that you say such spiteful things.   You are twenty-eight; you are first with nobody.   How can you bear to go on living?   What can you find to think about all day and all night?

JEM.   Think about?   Oh, sometimes my latter end, and sometimes my dinner!

LEN.   Poor old Jemima!

JEM.   It is a mercy one's palate outlives one's head.   One can still relish ice-cream when one has lost all appetite for moonshine.   (LENORE *starts to go out.*)

LEN.   Good-night, Jemima!   I am sorry I woke you; next time that I come to you for sympathy —

JEM.   Stay — stay!   Remember I was only half awake; I did not quite take it in.   I — I — dare say he is very nice when you come to know him.   He looks quite like a gentleman, has — very — good — teeth — I am sure — at least, I think — that he will improve on acquaintance.

LEN.   It is not of the least consequence *what* you think.

(*Exit.*)

JEM.   I suppose I was not sympathetic.   But he is poor; he is ugly; he is ill-tempered.   I could not marry a man who has any of those qualities, and that deluded girl is going to marry a man who has them all.   And just because she has " Fallen in Love "!

SCENE FROM "THE DAYS OF BRUCE."

BY GRACE AQUILAR.

CHARACTERS.

EARL OF BUCHAN.
LADY ISABELLA, *his wife.*
ALAN, *their son.*

(LADY ISABELLA *and* ALAN *seated in the hunting-lodge;*
noise without.)

ALAN. King Robert returned already! They must have had an unusually successful chase. I must e'en seek them and inquire.

(*Door is rudely flung open, and the* EARL OF BUCHAN *appears on the threshold.* ALAN *starts up and lays one hand on his sword, and places the other around his mother.*)

ALAN. Who and what art thou? What bold knight and honorable chevalier art thou, thus seeking by stealth the retreat of a wanderer, and overpowering by numbers and treachery men who on the field thou and such as thou had never dared to meet?

EARL. Thou hast a worthy tongue, my pretty springald; canst thou use thy sword as bravely? Who and what am I? Ask of the lady thou hast so caressingly encircled with thine arm; perchance she can give thee information.

ALAN. Mother, mother! speak to thy son. Why, why art thou thus? Who is this man?

EARL. Who and what am I? Wouldst thou know, Alan

of Buchan? Even a faithful knight, soldier, and subject of his Royal Highness, Edward, King of England and Scotland, and consequently thy foe; the insulted and dishonored husband of the woman thou callest mother, and consequently thy father, young man. Ha! have I spoken home? Thy sword, thy sword! Acknowledge thy loyalty to thy father and king, and for thee all may yet be well.

ALAN. Never! Never, Lord of Buchan! for father I cannot call thee. Thou mayest force me to resign my sword, thou mayest bring me to the block, but acknowledge allegiance to a foreign tyrant who hath no claims on Scotland or her sons, save those of hate and detestation, that thou canst never do, even if thy sword be pointed at my heart.

EARL. Boy! thou hast learned a goodly lesson of disobedience and daring, of a truth. The Lady Isabella deems, perchance, she has done her duty to her husband in placing a crown on the head of his hereditary and hated foe, and leading his son in the same path of rebellion and disloyalty.

LADY ISA. Earl of Buchan, I have done my duty alike to my country and my son. According to the dictates of my conscience, mine honor as a Scottish woman, the mother of a Scottish warrior, I have done my duty; and neither imprisonment, nor torture, nor death, will bid me retract those principles. Pardon me, my lord, but there is no rebellion in raising the standard against Edward. By what right is Edward of England King of Scotland? Lord of Buchan, I *have* done my duty. As my father taught *me*, I have taught my child.

EARL. Regarding, of course, madam, all which that child's father would have taught him. Oh, thou hast done well, most intrinsically well!

ALAN. We are in thy power, it is true. But hadst thou wished thy son to imbibe thy peculiar principles, to forget his country and her rights, it had been better, perchance, hadst thou remembered thou hadst a child. Had the duty of a father been performed, perchance I had not forgotten mine as a son! As it is, we stand as strangers and as foes. Against thee, in truth, I will not raise my sword, but further we are severed, and forever.

EARL. It is well, young man. I thank you for my freedom. As my *son*, I might stand between thee and Edward's wrath; as a stranger and my foe, why, whate'er his sentence be — the axe and block without doubt — let it work; it will move me little.

LADY ISA. Heed not his rash words, heed them not! Neglected, forgotten him as thou hast, yet, Lord of Buchan, he is still thy son. Oh, in mercy expose him not to the deadly wrath of Edward! No, no; it cannot be! thou wilt relent, thou wilt have mercy; let him but be free, and do with me even what thou wilt!

EARL. Free! go free! Let him go free, forsooth, when he tells me he is my foe, and will go hence and join my bitterest enemies the moment he is free. Go free! And who art thou who askest this boon? Hast thou such claims on me, that for thy pleasure I should give freedom to thy son?

LADY ISA. (*kneeling*). My lord, my lord, 'tis for thine own sake, for his, thy child as well as mine, I do beseech, implore thy mercy! Oh, is it not sufficient triumph to have in thy power thy wife, who hath dared thy authority, who hath joined the patriot band, and so drawn down on her the vengeance of Edward? The price of a traitor is set upon her head. Is not one victim enough? Will not my capture insure thee reward and honor in the court of Edward? Then do with me what thou wilt — chains, torture, death; but my child, my brave boy — oh, if thou hast one spark of mercy in thy heart, let him go!

ALAN. Mother, mother, this shalt not be! Look upon that face, and know thou pleadest in vain. I will not accept my freedom at such a price; thy knee, thy supplications unto

a heart of stone, for me! No, no, mother, dear mother; we
will die together! (*Raises* ISABELLA.)

EARL. Thou art a boy, a foolish boy! I will give thee
not freedom alone, but honor, station, and wealth; all on
one condition, so slight and simple that thou art worse than
fool an thou refusest.

ALAN. Speak on; I hear.

EARL. Give me but information of the movements of him
thou callest king.

ALAN (*starting up*). In other words, *betray him!* Oh,
shame, shame on thee, my lord! Honor, station, wealth!
Oh, knowest thou the human heart so little as to believe
these can exist with black treachery and remorse? Once
and forever, I tell thee no!

EARL. Beware! If the Bruce return not within forty-
eight hours, proud boy, and thou art silent still, thou diest.

LADY ISA. Thou shalt not, thou shalt not, my beloved!
Thy death will be on my head, though it come from a
father's hand. I will be heard. My lord, my lord, I ask
but his freedom, and of whom? Of his father, his own father.
Let him, oh, let him be free! Have mercy!

EARL. Mercy on thee, thou false and perjured woman!
Do I not know thee, minion? Do I not know thy motives
in leaving thy husband's castle for the court of Bruce?
Patriotism, ha! the patriotism that had vent in giving and
receiving love from him, the Bruce.

LADY ISA. Man!

EARL. Ha! faithless woman, thou bravest it well. I
know thee! I know that thou didst love him ere that false
hand and falser heart were given to me.

ALAN. Silence, false, blasphemous villain! 'Tis thou
who art false and faithless. (*Draws sword.*)

LADY ISA. Alan, I charge thee put up thy sword — it is
thy father.

ALAN. O God, my father speaks it, and I am powerless
to avenge.

LADY ISA.   I need not thy vengeance, my beloved. My
heart is known unto my God, my innocence to thee; his
blessing rest with thee.   Be firm; be thy noble self.   And
now a while farewell.   (*Goes toward door.*)

EARL.   Whither goest thou, madam?   Bold as thou art, it
is well to know thou art a prisoner, accused of high treason
against King Edward.

LADY ISA.   I need not your lordship's voice to give me
such information.

EARL.   Bid a last farewell to thy son, then; for an ye
part now, it is forever.   Ye see him not again.

LADY ISA.   Then be it so; we shall meet where falsehood
and malignant hate can never harm us more.   God bless
you, my son !

THE COUNTRY WIFE.

BY WILLIAM WYCHERLEY.

CHARACTERS.

MR. PINCHWIFE.
MRS. PINCHWIFE.

(*A room in* PINCHWIFE'S *house. Enter* MR. *and* MRS.
PINCHWIFE.)

PINCHWIFE.   Come, tell me, I say!

MRS. PINCHWIFE.   Lord! hain't I told it a hundred times
over?

PINCH. (*aside*).   I would try if in the repetition of the ungrateful tale I could find her altering it in the least circum-
stance; for if the story is false, she is so too. (*Aloud.*)
Come, how was't?

MRS. PINCH.   Lord! what pleasure you take to hear it,
sure!

PINCH.   No, you take more in telling it, I find; but
speak, how was't?

MRS. PINCH.   He kissed me a hundred times, and told
me he fancied he kissed my fine sister, meaning me, you
know, whom he said he loved with all his soul.

PINCH.   But what! you stood very still when he kissed
you?

MRS. PINCH.   Yes, I warrant you; would you have had
me discovered myself?   He's a proper, goodly, strong man;
'tis hard, let me tell you, to resist him.

PINCH. (*aside*).   So, 'tis plain she loves him; yet she has

15

not love enough to conceal it from me. I must strangle that little monster while I can deal with him. (*Aloud.*) Go fetch pen, ink, and paper out of the next room.

Mrs. Pinch. Yes, bud. (*Exit.*)

Pinch. Love! 'twas he first gave women their craft, their art of deluding.

(*Re-enter* Mrs. Pinchwife.)

Come, minx, sit down and write!

Mrs. Pinch. Ay, dear bud; but I can't do 't very well. But what should I write for?

Pinch. I'll have you write a letter to your lover.

Mrs. Pinch. O Lord! you do but jeer; sure you jest.

Pinch. I am not so merry. Come! write as I bid you.

Mrs. Pinch. What! do you think I am a fool?

Pinch. (*aside*). She's afraid I would not dictate any love to him, therefore she's unwilling. (*Aloud.*) But you had best begin.

Mrs. Pinch. Indeed, and indeed, but I won't; so I won't!

Pinch. Why?

Mrs. Pinch. Because he's in town; you may send for him if you will.

Pinch. Very well; you would have him brought to you. Is it come to this? I say, take the pen and write, or you'll provoke me.

Mrs. Pinch. Lord! what d'ye make a fool of me for? Don't I know that letters are never writ but from the country to London, and from London into the country? Now he's in town, and I am in town too; therefore I can't write to him, you know.

Pinch. (*aside*). So! I am glad it is no worse. (*Aloud.*) Yes, you may, when your husband bids you, write letters to people that are in town.

Mrs. Pinch. Oh, may I so? Then I'm satisfied.

PINCH. Come, begin : — " Sir " —

MRS. PINCH. Sha'n't I say, "Dear Sir"? You know one always says something more than bare " sir."

PINCH. Write as I bid you !

MRS. PINCH. "Sir" — (*Writes.*)

PINCH. "Though I suffered last night your nauseous, loathed kisses and embraces " — Write !

MRS. PINCH. Let me but put out "loathed."

PINCH. Write, I say !

MRS. PINCH. Well, then. (*Writes.*)

PINCH. Let's see, what have you writ? (*Takes paper and reads.*) "Though I suffered last night your kisses and embraces " — Impudent creature ! where is " nauseous " and " loathed " ?

MRS. PINCH. I can't abide to write such filthy words.

PINCH. Once more, write as I'd have you, and question it not, or I will spoil thy writing with this. I will stab out those eyes that cause my mischief. (*Holds up a penknife.*)

MRS. PINCH. O Lord ! I will.

PINCH. So — so — let's see now. (*Reads.*) "Though I suffered last night your nauseous, loathed kisses and embraces " — go on — "yet I would not have you presume that you shall ever repeat them " — (*She writes.*)

MRS. PINCH. I have writ it.

PINCH. On, then — " I then concealed myself from your knowledge to avoid your insolences " —

MRS. PINCH. So —

PINCH. "The same reason, now I am out of your hands."

MRS. PINCH. So —

PINCH. " Makes me own to you my unfortunate, though innocent, frolic of being in man's clothes " —

MRS. PINCH. So —

PINCH. " That you may evermore cease to pursue her, who hates and detests you " —

MRS. PINCH. So — heigh !

PINCH. What! do you sigh? — "detests you — as much as she loves her husband and her honor " —

MRS. PINCH. I vow, husband, he'll ne'er believe I should write such a letter.

PINCH. What! he'd expect a kinder from you? Come, now your name only.

MRS. PINCH. What! sha'n't I say, " Your most faithful, humble servant till death "?

PINCH. No, tormenting fiend! (*Aside.*) Her style, I find, would be very soft. (*Aloud.*) Come, wrap it up now, whilst I go fetch wax and a candle; and write on the backside, " For Mr. Horner." (*Exit.*)

MRS. PINCH. " For Mr. Horner." So; I am glad he has told me his name. Dear Mr. Horner! but why should I send thee a letter that will vex thee, and make thee angry with me? Well, I will not send it. But, then, my husband — but, oh, what if I writ at bottom my husband made me write it? Ay, but, then, my husband would see't. Can one have no shift? Ay, a Londoner would have had a hundred presently. Stay — what if I should write a letter, and wrap it up like this, and write upon't too? I'll try it, so I will; for I will not send this letter to poor Mr. Horner, come what will on't. " Dear, sweet Mr. Horner" — (*writes, and repeats what she writes*) — so — " my husband would have me send you a base, rude, unmannerly letter; but I won't " — so — " and would have me say to you, I hate you, poor Mr. Horner; but I won't tell a lie for him " — there — " but I must make haste before my husband comes; and now he has taught me to write letters, you shall have longer ones from me, who am, dear, dear, poor, dear Mr. Horner, your most humble friend, and servant to command till death, — Margery Pinchwife." Stay — now wrap up this just like t'other — so — now write " For Mr. Horner" — but, oh, what shall I do with it? For here comes my husband.

Enter PINCHWIFE.

PINCH. [illegible]

MRS PINCH. [illegible]

PINCH. [illegible]
would not have [illegible]

MRS PINCH. [illegible]

PINCH. [illegible]

MRS PINCH. [illegible]
there I have [illegible]
think me so [illegible]
so I will.

(Snatches the letter from him, corrects it in the first and in the second [illegible].)

PINCH. Nay, I believe you will [illegible] and other
things too, which I would not have you.

MRS PINCH. So I will [illegible] and I
think I have. There's my letter to Mr Horner since he
needs have me send letters to folks.

PINCH. 'Tis well, but I warrant you would not have it
go now?

MRS PINCH. Yes indeed but I would dear now.

PINCH. Well, you are a good girl then. Come, let me
lock you up in your chamber till I come back; and be sure
you come not within three strides of the window, when I am
gone, for I have a spy in the street. (*Exit* MRS PINCH-
WIFE; PINCHWIFE *locks the door.*) Now I have secured all
within, I'll deal with the foe without.

(Holds up letter. Exit.)

A WOMAN'S HEART.

From "Frederick the Great and His Friends.")

By L. MÜHLBACH.

CHARACTERS.

Princess Amelia.
Emperor Frederick.

PRINCESS AMELIA. What is it that the king will ask of me? What new mysterious horror rises up threateningly before me, and casts a shadow upon my future? (*Enter* Emperor Frederick; *she advances to meet him. He embraces her, and then seats her on the divan by him.*) My brother, now we are alone. And now allow me to make known my request at once — remember, you have promised to grant it.

EMPEROR FREDERICK. Amelia, have you no tender word of greeting, of warm home-love to say to me? Do you not know that five years have passed since we have seen each other alone and enjoyed that loving and confidential intercourse which becomes brother and sister?

AM. (*sadly*). I know, these five years are written on my countenance, and if they have not left wrinkles on my brow, they have pierced my heart with many sorrows, and left their shadows there. Look at me, my brother — am I the same sister Amelia?

FRED. No, no! You are pallid — your cheeks are hollow. But it is strange, I see this now for the first time. The fatigue of yesterday has exhausted you; that is all.

AM. No; you find me pallid and hollow-eyed to-day, because you see me without rouge. I have to-day for the first

20

time laid aside the mask of rosy youth and smiling indifference with which I conceal my face and heart from the world. You see me to-day as I really am; you shall know what I have suffered. Perhaps then you will be willing to grant my request. Listen, my brother. I —

FRED. (*laying his hand on her shoulder*). Stop, Amelia! Since I look on you, I fear you will ask me something not in my power to grant.

AM. You have given your promise, sire.

FRED. I will not withdraw it; but I ask you now to hear my prayer before you speak. Perhaps it may modify your request. I allow myself, therefore, solely in consideration of your own interest, to beg that I may speak first.

AM. You are king, sire, and have only to command.

FRED. (*rising*). I stand now before you, princess, not as a king, but as the ambassador of a king. Princess Amelia, the King of Denmark asks your hand, and I have given my consent. Your approval alone is wanting, and I think you will not refuse it.

AM. (*indifferently*). Have you finished, sire?

FRED. I have finished, and await your reply.

AM. Before I answer, let me make known my request. Perhaps it may modify yours; does your majesty allow me to speak?

FRED. Speak.

AM. (*with agitation*). Sire, I pray for pardon for the Baron Frederick von Trenck. (*Falling on her knees and clasping one of her brother's hands in both of hers.*) Sire, I pray for pardon for Baron Frederick von Trenck! (FREDERICK *dashes her hands away, and walks hastily up and down.* AMELIA *rises and steps in front of him.*) He is wretched because he is banished from his home; he is poor because his estates have been confiscated. Help him to obtain possession of his rights. Ah, sire, you see well how modest, how faint-hearted I have become. I ask no longer for happiness, I ask for gold; and I think, sire, we owe him this pitiful reparation for a life's happiness trodden under foot.

FRED. And if I do this, will you fulfil my wish? Will you become the wife of the King of Denmark? Ah, you are silent. Now, then, listen. On the day in which you enter your own realm as queen of Denmark, on that day will I recall Trenck to Berlin, and all shall be forgotten. Decide now, Amelia.

AM. Sire, you offer me a cruel alternative. I cannot accept your proposition; I cannot become the wife of the King of Denmark.

FRED. And why not?

AM. Because I have sworn solemnly, calling God to witness, that I will never become the wife of any other man than him I love — because I consider myself bound to God and to my conscience to fulfil this oath. As I cannot be the wife of Trenck, I will remain unmarried.

FRED. The wife of Trenck! the wife of a traitor! You have squandered your love upon a wretched object who has forgotten you.

AM. Sire, no abuse of the man I love

FRED. You love him still! You have wept and bewailed him, while he has shamefully betrayed and mocked you. Yes, look on me with those scornful, rebellious glances, you must and shall know all. I tell you he has betrayed not only you, but his king. But I have had him closely watched; I know all his intrigues and artifices. I know he has had a love affair with the young Countess Narischkin — that he continued his attentions long after her marriage. Do you believe that he thought of you when he received from this woman all her gold and diamonds, in order to smooth the way to their flight?

AM. Mercy, mercy! (*Sinking upon a chair.*) Cease, my brother. Do you not see that your words are killing me?

FRED. Do you still feel bound by your oath? Do you not know that he is a faithless traitor, and that he has forgotten you?

AM. Sire, I took my oath without conditions, and I will keep it faithfully till my death. You say that Trenck forgot me in his prosperity; well, then, sire, in his misfortune he has remembered me. In his wretchedness he has written and called upon me for aid. It shall not be said that I did not hear his voice — that I was not joyfully ready to serve him. I repeat my request, sire — pardon for Baron Trenck!

FRED. And I — I ask if you accept my proposition — if you will become the wife of the King of Denmark? and mark well, princess, this is the answer to your prayer.

AM. May God take pity on me! I cannot break my oath. You can force me to leave my vows unfulfilled — not to become the wife of the man I love — but you cannot force me to perjure myself. I should indeed be forsworn if I stepped before the altar with another man, and promise a love and faith which my heart could never know.

FRED. Princess Amelia, I give you four weeks' respite. Take counsel with your conscience, your understanding, and your honor. In four weeks I will come for your answer. If you dare still to oppose my will, I will yet fulfil my promise and grant the favor you ask of me. I will make proposals to Trenck to return to Prussia, and the inducements I offer will be so splendid he will not resist them. Let me once have him here, and it shall be my affair to hold fast to him. (*Exit* FREDERICK.)

AM. I must warn Trenck. He must never return to Prussia; if he does, he is lost.

CONFLICTING DOUBTS.

BY W. S. GILBERT.

CHARACTERS.

BELINDA.
MINNIE.

(*Drawing-room in* MINNIE'S *house. A plate of tarts and a bottle of wine on table. Enter* MISS TREHERNE *dressed in stately and funereal black. Speaks to some one outside.*)

BELINDA.   Say that one on whose devoted head the black sorrows of a lifetime have fallen, even as a funeral pall, craves a minute's interview with a dear old friend.   At last I'm in my darling's home, the home of the bright, blithe, carolling thing that lit, as with a ray of heaven's sunshine, the murky gloom of my miserable schooldays.   But what do I see? Tarts? Ginger wine? There are rejoicings of some kind afoot.   Alas! I am out of place here.   What have I in common with tarts?   Oh, I am ill-attuned to scenes of revelry!   (*Takes a tart and eats it.*)

(*Enter* MINNIE.)

MINNIE.   Belinda! (*They rush in each other's arms.*)

BEL.   Minnie! My own long-lost lamb! This is the first gleam of joy that has lighted my darksome course this many and many a day.   And in spite of the change that time and misery have brought upon me, you knew me at once! (*Eating the tarts all the time.*)

MIN.   Oh, I felt sure it was you, from the message.

24

BEL.   How wondrously fair you have grown! And this dress! Why, it is surely a bridal dress! Those tarts — that wine! Surely this is not your wedding-day?

MIN.   Yes, dear; I shall be married in half an hour.

BEL.   Oh, strange chance! ˮOh, unheard of coincidence! Married! And to whom?

MIN.   Oh, to my dearest love — my cousin, Mr. Cheviot Hill. Perhaps you know the name?

BEL.   I have heard of the Cheviot Hills, somewhere. Happy — strangely happy girl! You, at least, know your husband's name. (*Sits on sofa.*)

MIN. (*sits on sofa*). Oh yes; it's on all his pocket-hand-kerchiefs.

BEL.   It is much to know. I do not know mine.

MIN.   Have you forgotten it?

BEL.   No; I never knew it. It is a dark mystery. It may not be fathomed. It is buried in the fathomless gulf of the Eternal Past. There let it be.

MIN.   Oh, tell me about it, dear.

BEL.   It is a lurid tale. Three months since I fled from a hated one, who was to have married me. He pursued me. I confided my distress to a young and wealthy stranger. Acting on his advice, I declared myself to be his wife; he declared himself to be my husband. We were parted immediately afterwards, and we have never met since. But this took place in Scotland; and by the law of that remark‑ able country we are man and wife, though I didn't know it at the time.

MIN. (*rises*). What fun!

BEL. (*rises*). Fun! Say, rather, horror — distraction — chaos. I am rent with conflicting doubts. Perhaps he was already married; in that case I am a bigamist. Maybe he is dead; in that case I am a widow. Maybe he is alive; in that case I am a wife. What am I? Am I single? Am I married? Can I marry? Have I married? May I marry? Who am I? Where am I? What am I? What is my name? What is my condition in life? If I am married, to whom am I married? If I am a widow, how came I to be a widow, and whose widow came I to be? Why am I his widow? What did he die of? Did he leave me anything? if anything, how much, and is it saddled with conditions? Can I marry without forfeiting it? Have I a mother-in-law? Have I a family of step-children, and if so, how many, and what are their ages, sizes, names, and dispositions? These are questions that rack me night and day, and until they are settled, peace and I are not on terms! (*Crosses*).

MIN. Poor dear thing!

BEL. But enough of my selfish sorrows. (*Goes to table and takes another tart; MINNIE is annoyed at this.*) Tell me about the noble boy who is about to make you his. Has he any dross?

MIN. I don't know. (*Secretly removes tarts from centre table to table left, near to door.*) I never thought of asking. I'm such a goose. But papa knows.

BEL. Have those base and servile things called settlements been satisfactorily adjusted? (*Eating.*)

MIN. I don't know. It never occurred to me to inquire. But papa can tell you.

BEL. The same artless little soul!

MIN. (*standing so as to conceal tarts from Belinda*). Yes, I am *quite* artless — quite, quite (*t*)-artless. But now that you *are* here, you will stay and see me married.

BEL. I would willingly be a witness to my darling's joy, but this attire is, perhaps, scarcely in harmony with a scene of revelry.

MIN. Well, dear, you're not a cheerful object, and that's the truth.

BEL. And yet these charnel-house ways may serve to remind the thoughtless banqueters that they are but mortal.

MIN. I don't think it will be necessary to do that, dear. Papa's sherry will make *that* quite clear to them.

BEL. Then I will hie me home, and array me in garments of less sombre hue.

MIN. I think it would be better, dear. Those are the very things for a funeral; but this is a wedding.

BEL. I see very little difference between them. But it shall be as you wish (*crosses to left*), though I have worn nothing but black since my miserable marriage. Farewell, dearest Minnie. There is a breakfast, I suppose?

MIN. Yes, at dear Cheviot's house.

BEL. That is well; I shall return in time for it. Thank heaven I can still eat! (*Takes a tart from table at door left, and exit, followed by* MINNIE, *who expresses annoyance at* BELINDA'S *greediness.*)

THE LIGHT THAT FAILED.

By Rudyard Kipling.

CHARACTERS.

Dick Heldar.
Maisie.

(Dick Heldar *is sitting by the window with his chin on his chest. There are three unopened letters in his hand which he turns over and over.*)

Dick. Three letters from Maisie, and I can't read them. When she finds that I don't write, she'll stop writing. It's better so. I couldn't be of any use to her now. Shall I let her know that I am blind. I have fallen low enough already. I'm not going to beg for pity. Besides, it would be cruel to her. O Maisie, Maisie! (*Hearing the door open, he thrusts the letters in his pocket. Enter* Maisie.) Halloa, Torp! Is that you? I've been so lonely.

(Maisie *leans against the door, and puts one hand to her breast.*)

Dick (*puzzled and irritated*). Torp, is that you? They said you were coming.

Maisie (*in a strained whisper*). No; it's only me.

Dick (*composedly, without moving*). H'm! This is a new phenomenon. Darkness I'm getting used to; but I object to hearing voices. (*He rises, and feels his way across the room.* Maisie *puts out her hand mechanically, and it touches his chest. He steps back as if he had been shot.*) It's Maisie! What are you doing here?

Mai. I came — I came — to see you — please.

28

DICK. Won't you sit down, then? You see, I've had some bother with my eyes, and —

MAI. I know, I know! Why didn't you tell me?

DICK. I couldn't write.

MAI. You might have told Mr. Torpenhow.

DICK. What has he to do with my affairs?

MAI. He — he brought me from Vitry-sur-Marne. He thought I ought to see you.

DICK. Why, what has happened? Can I do anything for you? No, I can't. I forgot.

MAI. O Dick, I'm so sorry! I've come to tell you, and — let me take you back to your chair.

DICK. Don't! I'm not a child. You only do that out of pity. I never meant to tell you anything about it. I'm no good now. I'm down and done for. Let me alone! (*Gropes his way back to the chair.*)

MAI. (*sitting on arm of his chair*). I sha'n't! You belong, now, Dickie, and I've come up all these stairs, and — and — and — Dick, you aren't going to be selfish, now I've come back? I'm so sorry! Oh, I'm so sorry!

DICK. I knew that was all. Won't you leave me alone! I shall have to suffer for this afterward.

MAI. You won't! (*Bends down and whispers in his ear.*) Yes, I do. My darling, I do. I don't care; you can sulk as much as you like and I won't be angry. I've been a villain —a wicked little villain. Shall I go down on my knees and tell you so? Don't be stupid, Dickie. It's no use pretending. You know you care for me.

DICK. I do! God knows I do.

MAI. What nonsense, then, pretending to be selfish! (*Her voice growing unsteady.*) D'you remember the Dover boat? (*Kissing him.*) Take that, then, and be sensible. Oh, help me, Dick! I can't make love all by myself. (*Bursts into tears. DICK putting his arms around her and stroking her head on his shoulder.*)

DICK. Hush, dear, hush! What's the use of worrying? It's all right now.

MAI. We did belong, Dick, didn't we. It was all my fault — all my fault.

DICK. I like that fault. Be more faultsome.

MAI. 'Course you did. (*Laughing.*) I — I had to do all the — the love-making. It was horrible!

DICK. It was only me; what did it matter? If it had been a strange man you might have objected. And then, again, you took me on my blind side.

MAI. That's an ugly word, and you aren't going to use it any more.

DICK. But it's true, dear. I'd give anything, except you, to see your face again. But I'm blind.

MAI. That's nonsense, too. You said ten years were nothing. And they weren't. We belonged just the same. Now, do you remember out on the flats, when my hair got into your eyes? (*Shaking down her hair, and letting it fall over his face.*) You couldn't see now if you tried ever so. Let's pretend it's only my hair in your eyes for just a little longer — fifty or sixty years. Fifty's five times less important than ten. Can't you see that, darling?

DICK (*contentedly*). I see. Oh, it's good to have you back again, Maisie!

MAI. It's gooder to be back, bad boy.

HOW SHE WON THE DIAMONDS.

(A Scene from " Weeping Wives.")

FROM THE FRENCH OF MESSRS. GIRAUDIN AND LAMBERT THIBOUST.

CHARACTERS.

CLOTILDE.
DELPHINE.

(Enter CLOTILDE, *centre.)*

DELPHINE.   Clotilde !

CLOTILDE.   Delphine !   *(They embrace and sit.)*

DEL.   Now, my dear Clotilde, tell me all about your marriage.

CLO.   It's your turn first.   You have much more experience, for you left the convent three years before me, recollect.

DEL.   True; I am getting old.   Well, Clotilde dear, I had scarcely left the convent, where we had such a perfectly blissful time, when I married.

CLO.   Yes; you married Albert's friend?

DEL.   Mr. Chambly?   Oh, no!   So you never heard it?   When Mr. Chambly married me *(very gayly)* I was already a widow.

CLO.   Two husbands in such a little while?   But you always were a clever creature.

DEL.   Yes — widow of Mr. Varenne — with whom I had not a happy time, and I was involved in lawsuits —   Well, no matter.   It left me with no inclination to marry again.   But Mr. Chambly is so good — oh, the best of men !   Well,

31

what could you expect? I am young — I dreaded solitude and *ennui* — I accepted him.

CLO. You are very wise, my dear. As for myself, what can I tell you, but that I am Albert's wife.

DEL. The sum of all earthly happiness.

CLO. He is too lovely — but —

DEL. Yes — distingué. What are you looking at?

CLO. Your diamond earrings.

DEL. Pretty, are they not? I got them yesterday at Mellerio's.

CLO. Ah! (*Sighs.*)

DEL. What do you mean by that tone? If you like them, there is another pair exactly like these.

CLO. (*sadly*). I know it.

DEL. Ask your husband for them.

CLO. (*with pathos*). I have already done so.

DEL. Well?

CLO. Nothing; let us talk of something else.

DEL. Not a bit; let's talk about the earrings.

CLO. (*reluctantly*). Well — Albert said — that is, he intimated that —

DEL. He refused you?

CLO. (*sighing*). Yes.

DEL. (*tragically*). My child, you are lost!

CLO. Lost?

DEL. Refused! And you allow your husband to place himself on such a footing in three months after marriage! (*Rises.*) Clotilde, you are on the verge of a bottomless abyss!

CLO. (*rising*). How you frighten me!

DEL. Your happiness depends on the first days of your married life. Ah! my dear, it was your lucky star that led you to me. If you want those diamonds you *must* have them. There!

CLO. But I have told you that Albert has declined to give them to me. I have already begged.

DEL.   In a sweet voice — with a tender look — and hanging upon his arm?

CLO.   Yes; the very best I could.

DEL.   All — are you sure? For winning a favor there is a certain arsenal of female coquetry, a certain look, accompanied by a certain little pouting — see — like this — hands clasped — head slightly inclined — a pleading voice — now observe — "Albert, my own Albert, can you refuse me what I ask?"

CLO.   I think I might do that.   (*Doubtfully.*)

DEL.   Try!

CLO. (*imitating her*).   "Albert, my own Albert, can you refuse me what I ask?"

DEL.   No; that is not a success: try again.

CLO.   How discouraging! Is there no other way? I can't pretend.

DEL.   I must think — Yes! I have it! Can you cry?

CLO. (*curiously*). Cry?

DEL.   You must learn to weep — why, all women know how to weep! You see, my dear Clotilde, between ourselves, men are not half as hard and wicked as we make them out, and when they see us weep they cannot resist us.

CLO. (*gayly*).   I never thought of that.

DEL.   M. Varenne, my first husband, was a perfect tyrant — I wept — and he was at my feet. Try it with M. de Rieux, and you will be astonished at the result.

CLO.   My good Delphine!

DEL.   The eloquence of tears is infallible. You will see.

CLO.   But how can one cry when there is nothing to cry about?

DEL.   Just get up the show. Put your handkerchief to your eyes, and the tears will come of themselves — Your husband.

GUINEVERE.

BY ALFRED TENNYSON.

CHARACTERS.

QUEEN GUINEVERE.
A NOVICE.

(QUEEN GUINEVERE *had fled the court, and sat*
There in the holy house at Almesbury
Weeping, none with her save a little maid,
A novice.)

NOVICE.   Late! so late!   What hour I wonder now?
(*Hums*).   Late, so late!—
   GUINEVERE.   O maiden, if indeed ye list to sing,
Sing, and unbind my heart, that I may weep.
   Nov. (*sings*).   "Late, late, so late! and dark the night
      and chill!
Late, late, so late! but ye can enter still.
Too late, too late! ye cannot enter now.

No light had we: for that we do repent;
And learning this, the bridegroom will relent.
Too late, too late! ye cannot enter now.

No light: so late! and dark and chill the night!
O let us in, that we may find the light!
Too late, too late: ye cannot enter now.

Have we not heard the bridegroom is so sweet?
O let us in, tho' late, to kiss his feet!

34

No, no, too late ! ye cannot enter now." —
O pray you, noble lady, weep no more ;
But let my words, the words of one so small,
But knowing nothing knows but to obey,
And if I do not there is penance given —
Comfort your sorrows ; for they do not flow
From evil done ; right sure am I of that,
Who see your tender grace and stateliness.
But weigh your sorrows with our lord the King's,
And weighing find them less ; for gone is he
To wage grim war against Sir Lancelot there,
Round that strong castle where he holds the Queen ;
And Modred, whom he left in charge of all,
The traitor — Ah, sweet lady, the King's grief
For his own self, and his own Queen, and realm,
Must needs be thrice as great as any of ours.
For me, I thank the saints, I am not great.
For if there ever come a grief to me
I cry my cry in silence, and have done.
None knows it, and my tears have brought me good :
But even were the griefs of little ones
As great as those of great ones, yet this grief
Is added to the griefs the great must bear,
That howsoever much they may desire
Silence, they cannot weep behind a cloud :
As even the good King and his wicked Queen,
And were I such a King with such a Queen,
Well might I wish to veil her wickedness,
But were I such a King, it could not be.
   GUIN. (*aside*).   Will the child kill me with her innocent
    talk ?
(*Aloud*.)   Must not I,
If this false traitor have displaced his lord,
Grieve with the common grief of all the realm ?
   Nov.   Yea, this is all woman's grief,

That *she* is woman, whose disloyal life
Hath wrought confusion in the Table Round
Which good King Arthur founded, years ago,
With signs and miracles and wonders, there
At Camelot, ere the coming of the Queen.
   GUIN. (*aside*).   Will the child kill me with her innocent
     prate?
(*Aloud.*)   O little maid, shut in by nunnery walls,
What canst thou know of Kings and Table Round,
Or what of signs and wonders, but the signs
And simple miracles of thy nunnery?
   Nov.   Yea, but I know; the land was full of signs
And wonders ere the coming of the Queen.
So said my father, and himself was knight
Of the great Table — at the founding of it;
And rode thereto from Lyonnesse, and he said
That as he rode, an hour or may be twain
After the sunset, down the coast, he heard
Strange music, and he paused, and turning — there,
All down the lonely coast of Lyonnesse,
Each with a beacon-star upon his head,
And with a wild sea-light about his feet,
He saw them — headland after headland flame
Far on into the rich heart of the west:
And in the light the white mermaiden swam,
And strong man-breasted things stood from the sea,
And sent a deep sea-voice thro' all the land,
To which the little elves of chasm and cleft
Made answer, sounding like a distant horn.
So said my father — yea, and furthermore,
Next morning while he passed the dim-lit woods,
Himself beheld three spirits mad with joy
Come dashing down on a tall wayside flower,
That shook beneath them, as the thistle shakes
When three gray linnets wrangle for the seed:

And still at evenings on before his horse
The flickering fairy-circle wheeled and broke
Flying, and linked again, and wheeled and broke
Flying, for all the land was full of life.
And when at last he came to Camelot,
A wreath of airy dancers hand-in-hand
Swung round the lighted lanterns of the hall:
And in the hall itself was such a feast
As never man had dream'd: for every knight
Had whatsoever meat he long'd for served
By hands unseen; and even as he said
Down in the cellars merry bloated things
Shoulder'd the spiggot, straddling on the butts
While the wine ran: so glad were spirits and men
Before the coming of the Queen.

   GUIN. Were they so glad? ill prophets were they all,
Spirits and men; could none of them foresee,
Not even thy wise father with his signs
And wonders, what has fall'n upon the realm?

   Nov. Yea, one, a bard; of whom my father said,
Full many a noble war-song had he sung.
Ev'n in the presence of an enemy's fleet,
Between the steep cliff and the coming wave,
And many a mystic lay of life and death
Had chanted on the smoky mountain tops,
When round him bent the spirits of the hills
With all their dewy hair blown back like flame:
So said my father — and that night the bard
Sang Arthur's glorious wars, and sang the King
As wellnigh more than man, and rail'd at those
Who call'd him the false son of Gorloïs:
For there was no man knew from whence he came
But after tempest, when the long wave broke
All down the thundering shores of Bude and Bos,
There came a day as still as heaven, and then

They found a naked child upon the sands
Of dark Tintagil, by the Cornish sea;
And that was Arthur; and they foster'd him
Till he by miracle was approven king:
And that his grave should be a mystery
From all men, like his birth, and could he find
A woman in her womanhood as great
As he was in his manhood, then, he sang,
The twain together well might change the world.
But even in the middle of his song
He falter'd, and his hand fell from the harp,
And pale he turn'd, and reel'd, and would have fall'n,
But that they stay'd him up; nor would he tell
His vision; but what doubt that he foresaw
This evil work of Lancelot and the Queen?
    GUIN. (*aside*).   Lo! they have set her on,
Our simple-seeming Abbess and her nuns,
To play upon me.   (*Bows her head.*)
    Nov.   Shame on my garrulity!
The good nuns check my gadding tongue full often.
And, sweet lady, if I seem
To vex an ear too sad to listen to me,
Unmannerly, with prattling and the tales
Which my good father told me, check me too,
Nor let me shame my father's memory, one
Of noblest manners, tho' himself would say
Sir Lancelot had the noblest; and he died,
Kill'd in a tilt, come next five summers back,
And left me; but of others who remain,
And of the two first-famed for courtesy —
And pray you check me if I ask amiss —
But pray you, which had noblest, while you moved
Among them, Lancelot or our lord the King?
    GUIN.   Sir Lancelot as became a noble knight,
Was gracious to all ladies, and the same

In open battle or the tilting-field
Forbore his own advantage, and the King
In open battle or the tilting-field
Forbore his own advantage, and these two
Were the most nobly-mannered men of all;
For manners are not idle, but the fruit
Of loyal natures, and of noble mind.

   Nov. Yea, be manners such fair fruit?
Then Lancelot needs must be a thousand-fold
Less noble, being, as all rumor runs,
The most disloyal friend in all the world.

   Guin. O closed about by narrowing nunnery-walls,
What knowest thou of the world, and all its lights
And shadows, all the wealth and all the woe?
If ever Lancelot, that most noble knight,
Were for one hour less noble than himself,
Pray for him that he scape the doom of fire,
And weep for her who drew him to his doom.

   Nov. Yea, I pray for both;
But I should all as soon believe that his,
Sir Lancelot's, were as noble as the King's,
As I could think, sweet lady, yours would be
Such as they are, were you the sinful Queen.

   Guin. Such as thou art, be never maiden more
For ever! thou their tool, set on to plague
And play upon, and harry me, petty spy
And traitress. — Get thee hence.   (*Exit* Novice.)
The simple, fearful child
Meant nothing, but my own too-fearful guilt,
Simpler than any child, betrays itself. —
But help me, heaven, for surely I repent.
For what is true repentance but in thought, —
Not even in inmost thought to think again
The sin that made the past so pleasant to us:
And I have sworn never to see him more,
To see him more.

SCENE FROM "IVANHOE."

BY SIR WALTER SCOTT.

CHARACTERS.

ROWENA, *wife to* IVANHOE.
REBECCA, *a Jewess in love with* IVANHOE.

(*The second morning after the wedding* LADY ROWENA *receives a message that a damsel desires admission to her presence, and wishes to speak with her alone. She hesitates, and then sends word to admit her.* REBECCA *enters veiled.* ROWENA *rises, and starts to conduct her visitor to a seat, but* REBECCA *kneels, and kisses the hem of* ROWENA'S *tunic.*)

ROWENA. What means this, lady? Why do you offer me a deference so unusual?

REBECCA. Because to you, Lady of Ivanhoe (*rises*), I may lawfully, and without rebuke, pay the debt of gratitude which I owe to Wilfred of Ivanhoe. I am (*raises veil*) — forgive the boldness which has offered to you the homage of my country — I am the unhappy Jewess for whom your husband hazarded his life against such fearful odds in the tilt-yard of Templestone.

Row. Damsel, Wilfred of Ivanhoe on that day rendered back but in slight measure your unceasing charity towards him in his wounds and misfortunes. Speak! Is there aught remains in which he or I can serve thee?

REB. Nothing; unless you will transmit to him my grateful farewell.

Row. You leave England, then?

Reb. I leave it, lady, ere this moon again changes. My father hath a brother high in favor with Mohammed Boabdil, King of Grenada. Thither we go, secure of peace and protection.

Row. And are you not then as well protected in England? My husband has favor with the king — the king himself is just and generous.

Reb. Lady, I doubt it not; but the people of England are a fierce race, quarrelling ever with their neighbors or among themselves. Such is no safe abode for the children of my people. Not in a land of war and blood can Israel hope to rest during her wanderings.

Row. But you, maiden, — you surely can have nothing to fear. She who nursed the sick-bed of Ivanhoe — she can have nothing to fear in England, where Saxon and Norman will contend to do her honor.

Reb. Thy speech is fair, lady, and thy purpose fairer; but it may not be — there is a gulf betwixt us. Our breeding, our faith, alike forbid either to pass over it. Farewell — yet, ere I go, indulge me one request. The bridal-veil hangs over thy face; deign to raise it, and let me see the features of which fame speaks so highly.

Row. They are scarce worthy of being looked upon; but I will remove the veil. (*Takes it off.*)

Reb. Lady, your countenance will long remain in my remembrance. There reigns in it gentleness and goodness. Long, long will I remember your features, and bless God that I leave my noble deliverer united with — (*Stops short; hastily wipes her eyes.*) I am well, lady — well, but my heart swells when I think of the lists at Templestone. Farewell. One, the most trifling, part of my duty remains undischarged. Accept this casket — startle not at its contents. (Rowena *opens casket, and then holds it out to* Rebecca.)

Row. It is impossible. I dare not accept a gift of such consequence.

REB. Yet keep it, lady. *You* have power, rank, command, influence; *we* have wealth, the source both of our strength and weakness; the value of these toys ten times multiplied would not influence half as much as your slightest wish. To you, therefore, the gift is of little value. Accept them, lady — to me they are valueless. I will never wear jewels more.

ROW. You are then unhappy ! Oh, remain with us — the counsel of wise men will wean you from your erring law, and I will be a sister to you.

REB. No, lady, that may not be. I may not change the faith of my fathers like a garment unsuited to the climate in which I seek to dwell, and unhappy, lady, I will not be. He to whom I dedicate my future life will be my comforter, if I do his will.

ROW. Have you then convents, to one of which you mean to retire?

REB. No, lady; but among our people, since the time of Abraham downwards, have been women who have devoted their thoughts to Heaven, and their actions to works of kindness to men, tending the sick, feeding the hungry, and relieving the distressed. Among these will Rebecca be numbered. Say this to thy lord should he chance to inquire after the fate of her whose life he saved. Farewell, and may He who made both Jew and Christian shower down on you His choicest blessings ! The bark that wafts us hence will be under weigh ere we can reach the port. (*Exit.*)

THE PARTING OF HECTOR AND ANDROMACHE.

BY HOMER.

CHARACTERS.

HECTOR.
ANDROMACHE.

HECTOR.   This time forbids to rest;
The Trojan bands, by hostile fury press'd,
Demand their Hector, and his arm require;
The combat urges, and my soul's on fire.
Ere yet I mingle in the direful fray,
My wife, my infant, claim a moment's stay;
This day (perhaps the last that sees me here)
Demands a parting word, a tender tear:
This day, some god who hates our Trojan land
May vanquish Hector by a Grecian hand.

(*Enter* ANDROMACHE.)

ANDROMACHE.   Too daring prince!   Ah, whither dost
    thou run?
Ah, too forgetful of thy wife and son!
And think'st thou not how wretched we shall be
A widow I, a helpless orphan he?
For sure such courage length of life denies,
And thou must fall, thy virtue's sacrifice.
O grant me, gods, ere Hector meets his doom,
All I can ask of Heaven, an early tomb

43

So shall my days in one sad tenor run,
And end with sorrows as they first begun.
No parent now remains my grief to share,
No father's aid, no mother's tender care.
The fierce Achilles wrapt our walls in fire,
Laid Thebè waste, and slew my warlike sire!
By the same arm my seven brave brothers fell;
My mother lived to wear the victor's bands,
The queen of Hippoplacia's sylvan lands:
Redeem'd too late, she scarce beheld again
Her pleasing empire and her native plain,
When ah! oppress'd by life-consuming woe,
She fell a victim to Diana's bow.

   Yet while my Hector still survives, I sée
My father, mother, brethren, all, in thee;
Alas! my parents, brothers, kindred, all
Once more will perish if my Hector fall,
Thy wife, thy infant, in thy danger share:
Oh, prove a husband's and a father's care!
That quarter most the skilful Greeks annoy,
Where yon wild fig-trees join the walls of Troy.
Thou, from this tower defend the important post,
There Agamemnon points his dreadful host.
Let others in the field their arms employ,
But stay my Hector here, and guard his Troy.

   HEC.   That post shall be my care,
Not that alone, but all the works of war.
How would the sons of Troy, in arms renown'd,
And Troy's proud dames, whose garments sweep the ground
Attaint the lustre of my former name,
Should Hector basely quit the field of fame?
My early youth was bred to martial pains,
My soul impels me to the embattled plains!
Let me be foremost to defend the throne,
And guard my father's glories, and my own.

Yet come it will, the day decreed by fates !
(How my heart trembles while my tongue relates!)
The day when thou, imperial Troy! must bend,
And see thy warriors fall, thy glories end.
And yet no dire presage so wounds my mind,
As thine, Andromache !   Thy griefs I dread :
I see thee trembling, weeping, captive led!
In Argive looms our battles to design,
And woes, of which so large a part was thine !
There while you groan beneath the load of life,
They cry, " Behold the mighty Hector's wife !"
Some haughty Greek, who lives thy tears to see,
Imbitters all thy woes, by naming me.
May I lie dead before that dreadful day,
Press'd with a load of monumental clay !
Thy Hector wrapt in everlasting sleep,
Shall neither hear thee sigh, nor see thee weep.
　Andromache ! my soul's far better part,
Why with untimely sorrow heaves thy heart?
No hostile hand can antedate my doom
Till fate condemns me to the silent tomb.
No force can then resist, no flight can save,
All sink alike, the fearful and the brave.
No more — but hasten to thy tasks at home,
There guide the spindle, and direct the loom :
Me glory summons to the martial scene,
The field of combat is the sphere for men.
Where heroes war, the foremost place I claim,
The first in danger as the first in fame.

HER EVIL GENIUS.

(From " The New Magdalen.")

BY WILKIE COLLINS.

CHARACTERS.

GRACE ROSEBERRY.
MERCY MERRICK.

(GRACE ROSEBERRY *seated.   Enter* MERCY MERRICK, *and advances rapidly.*   GRACE *stops her with a warning hand; she starts to take a chair to support herself.*)

GRACE.   I forbid you to be seated in my presence.   You have no right to be in this house at all.   Remember, if you please, who I am, and who you are !

MERCY (*lifting her head suddenly to speak, but checking herself; aside*).   I will be worthy of Julian Gray's confidence in me.   I will bear anything from the woman I have wronged. (*Aloud.*) Oh, you do not know the temptation that tried me when the shell struck you down in the French cottage ! There you lay — dead !   *Your* name was untainted.   *Your* future promised me the reward which had been denied the honest efforts of a penitent woman.   The possibility of personating you forced itself upon my mind.   Impulsively, recklessly, wickedly, I seized the opportunity.   I took your papers, the letter to Lady Janet Roy, and came here.

GRACE.   And I have got you at last, Mercy Merrick. Thank God, my turn has come !   You can't escape me now !

MERCY.   I have not avoided you.   I would have gone to you of my own accord if I had known that you were here.

46

It is my heart-felt wish to own that I have sinned against you, and to make all the atonement that I can. I am too anxious to deserve your forgiveness to have any fear of seeing you.

GRACE (*furiously*).   How dare you speak to me as if you were my equal ? You stand there and answer me as if you had your right and your place in this house. You audacious woman ! I have my right and my place here — and what am I obliged to do ? I am obliged to hang about in the grounds, and fly from the sight of the servants, and hide like a thief, and all for what ? For the chance of having a word with *you*. Yes, you ! madam ! With the air of the Refuge and the dirt of the streets on you !

MERCY.   If it is your pleasure to use hard words to me, I have no right to resent them.

GRACE.   You have no right to anything. You have no right to the gown on your back. Look at yourself, and look at *me*. Who gave you that dress ? Who gave you those jewels ? I know ! Lady Janet gave them to Grace Roseberry. Are *you* Grace Roseberry ? That dress is mine. Take off your jewels. They were meant for me.

MERCY.   You may soon have them, Miss Roseberry. They will not be in my possession many hours longer.

GRACE.   What do you mean ?

MERCY.   However badly you may use me, it is my duty to undo the harm I have done. I am bound to do you justice. I am determined to confess the truth.

GRACE (*smiling scornfully*).   You confess ! Do you think I am fool enough to believe that ? You are one shameful, brazen lie from head to foot ! Are *you* the woman to give up your silks and your jewels, and your position in this house, and to go back to the Refuge of your own accord ? No, no ! you are of the sort that cheat and lie to the last. I am glad of it ; I shall have the joy of exposing you myself before the whole house. I shall be the blessed means of casting you back on the streets. Oh! it will be almost worth all I have gone through to see you with a policeman's arm on your hand, and the mob pointing at you and mocking you on your way to jail.

MERCY. Miss Roseberry, I have borne without a murmur the bitterest words you could say to me. Spare me any more insults. Indeed, indeed — I am resolved to confess everything!

GRACE (*contemptuously*). You are not far from the bell; ring it. (*Satirically.*) You are a perfect picture of repentance — you are dying to own the truth. Call in Lady Janet, — call in Mr. Gray — call in the servants. Go down on your knees, and acknowledge yourself an impostor before them all. Then I will believe you — not before.

MERCY. Don't, don't turn me against you!

GRACE. What do I care whether you are against me or not?

MERCY. Don't — don't for your own sake, go on provoking me much longer.

GRACE. For my own sake? You insolent creature! Do you mean to threaten me?

MERCY. Have some compassion on me. Badly as I have behaved to you, I am still a woman like yourself. I can't face the shame of acknowledging what I have done before the whole house. Lady Janet treats me like a daughter. I can't tell her to her face that I have cheated her out of her love. But she shall know it for all that. I can, I will, before I rest to-night, tell the whole truth to Mr. Julian Gray.

GRACE (*laughing cynically*). Aha! Now we have come to it at last.

MERCY. No more, Miss Roseberry! You have tortured me enough already.

GRACE. Mr. Julian Gray! I was behind the billiard-room door; I saw you coax Mr. Julian Gray to come in! Confession becomes quite a luxury with Mr. Julian Gray!

MERCY. Take care! Take care!

GRACE. You haven't been on the streets for nothing. Ah! you sicken me. *I'll* see that his eyes are opened; he shall know who you are.

MERCY (*with suppressed fury*). Who are *you?* (GRACE *starts up.*) I remember! You are the madwoman from the hospital. I am not afraid of you. Sit down and rest yourself, Mercy Merrick.

GRACE. What does this mean?

MERCY. It means that I recall every word I said to you just now. It means that I am resolved to keep my place in this house.

GRACE. Are you out of your senses?

MERCY. You are not far from the bell. Ring it! Do what you asked *me* to do. Call in the household, and ask which of us is mad — you or I?

GRACE. You can't send for them. You dare not!

MERCY. I can and dare. You have not a shadow of proof against me. I mean to deserve your opinion of me — I will keep my dresses and my jewels and my position in the house. I deny that I have done wrong. I deny that I have injured you. How was I to know you would come to life again? Have I degraded your name and your character? I have done honor to both. I have won everybody's liking and everybody's respect. Do you think Lady Janet would have loved you as she loves me? I tell you to your face, I have filled the false position more creditably than you have filled the true one, and I mean to keep it. I am Grace Roseberry; and you are Mercy Merrick. Disprove it if you can! I won't give up your name; I won't restore your character! Do your worst; I defy you! (*Exit.*)

GRACE. You defy me? You won't defy me long, Mercy Merrick! You shall repent this to the last hour of your life!

ANTIGONE.

By Sophocles.

CHARACTERS.

ANTIGONE, *daughter to* ŒDIPUS.
ISMENE, *sister to* ANTIGONE.

(ANTIGONE *was the daughter of* ŒDIPUS. *When her father, after discovering that he had killed his father, and married his mother, put out his eyes in despair, and resigned the throne of Thebes,* ANTIGONE *guided him on his way, and attended to him until his death. Her brothers having fallen in war by each other's hand, for the possession of Thebes, and she having attempted to bury* POLYNICES *in defiance of a decree, she was sentenced to be buried alive in a vault.*)

ANTIGONE.   O, my dear sister, my best beloved Ismene!
Is there an evil, by the wrath of Jove
Reserved for Œdipus' unhappy race,
We have not felt already?   Sorrow and shame,
And bitterness and anguish, all that's sad,
All that's distressful, hath been ours, and now   ·
This dreadful edict from the tyrant comes
To double our misfortunes.   Hast thou heard
What harsh commands he hath imposed on all,
Or art thou still to know what future ills
Our foes have yet in store to make us wretched?
ISMENE.   Since that unhappy day, Antigone,
When by each other's hand our brothers fell,
And Greece dismissed her armies, I have heard
Naught that could give or joy or grief to me.

50

ANT.   I thought thou wert a stranger to the tidings,
And therefore called thee forth, that here alone,
I might impart them to thee.
ISM.   Oh, what are they?
For something dreadful labors in thy breast.
ANT.   Know then, from Creon, our indulgent lord,
Our hapless brothers met a different fate:
To honor one, and one to infamy
He hath consigned.   With funeral rites he graced
The body of our dear Eteocles,
Whilst Polynices' wretched carcass lies
Unburied, unlamented, left exposed
A feast for hungry vultures on the plain.
No pitying friend will dare to violate
The tyrant's harsh command, for public death
Awaits th' offender.   Creon comes himself
To tell us of it — such is our condition.
This is the crisis, this the hour, Ismene,
That must declare thee worthy of thy birth,
Or show thee mean, base, degenerate.
   ISM.   What wouldst thou have me do? — defy his
      power?
Contemn the laws?
   ANT.   Consider and resolve.   To act with me, or not.
   ISM.   What daring deed
Wouldst thou attempt?   What is it?   Speak!
   ANT.   To join
And take the body, my Ismene.
   ISM.   Ha!
And wouldst thou dare to bury it, when thus
We are forbidden?
   ANT.   Aye, to bury him!
He is my brother, and thine too, Ismene;
Therefore, consent or not, I have determined
I'll not disgrace my birth.

Ism.   Hath not the king
Pronounced it death to all?

Ant.   He hath no right,
No power to keep me from my own.

Ism.   Alas!
Remember our unhappy father's fate:
His eyes torn out by his own fatal hand,
Oppressed with shame and infamy he died;
Fruit of his crimes! a mother, and a wife —
Dreadful alliance! — self-devoted, fell;
And last, in one sad day, Eteocles
And Polynices by each other slain.
Left as we are, deserted and forlorn,
What from our disobedience can we hope
But misery and ruin? Poor weak women,
Helpless, nor formed by nature to contend
With powerful man? We are his subjects too.
Therefore to this, and worse than this, my sister,
We must submit.
Since to attempt what we can never hope
To execute, is folly all and madness.

Ant.   Wert thou to proffer what I do not ask —
Thy poor assistance — I would scorn it now.
Act as thou wilt; I'll bury him myself;
Let me perform but that, and death is welcome:
I'll do the pious deed, and lay me down
By my dear brother. Thou, meantime,
What the gods hold most precious mayst despise.

Ism.   I reverence the gods; but, in defiance
Of laws, and unassisted to do this,
It were most dangerous.

Ant.   That be thy excuse,
Whilst I prepare the funeral pile.

Ism.   Alas!
I tremble for thee.

ANT.   Tremble for thyself,
And not for me.

ISM.   Oh ! do not tell thy purpose,
I beg thee, do not !   I shall not betray thee.

ANT.   I'd have it known; and I shall hate thee more
For thy concealment, than, if loud to all,
Thou wouldst proclaim the deed.

ISM.   Thou hast a heart
Too daring, and ill-suited to thy fate.

ANT.   I know my duty, and I'll pay it there
Where 'twill be best accepted.

ISM.   Couldst thou do it !
But 'tis not in thy power.

ANT.   When I know that
It will be time to quit my purpose.

ISM.   It cannot be ; 'tis folly to attempt it.

ANT.   Go on, and I shall hate thee !   Our dead brother,
He too shall hate thee as his bitterest foe ;
Go, leave me here to suffer for my rashness ;
Whate'er befalls, it cannot be so dreadful
As not to die with honor ?

ISM.   Then, farewell,
Since thou wilt have it so; and know, Ismene
Pities thy weakness, but admires thy virtue.

FRED'S FIANCÉE.

By Alice E. Ives.

(In the New York Recorder.)

CHARACTERS.

Mrs. John Taxton, *a society woman.*
Mrs. Stuart Bidderby, *also a society woman, rather younger than* Mrs.
Taxton.
Miss Dexter, *small, slight, blue-eyed, and light-haired.*

(Scene.— *A drawing-room in* Mrs. Taxton's *house. Tea-table, with tea-service, right. Couches at left, palms, pictures, all showing luxury and good taste. A pile of photographs on table near centre. Window at back.* Mrs. Taxton *discovered comfortably ensconced on couch reading a letter.*)

Mrs. Taxton (*looking up from letter and laughing*). Well, of all things! Fred engaged! The rascal! To be so sly about it! (*Hears sound outside, starts, and listens.*) A carriage! (*Gets up and looks out of window.*) Mrs. Bidderby; I'll have some fun telling her about it. She used to flirt outrageously with Fred. Always thought she cared for him, too. Who's that coming with her? Not much style — young, though, and rather pretty; some country cousin, I'll wager, and she's showing her the sights. I'm one, I suppose. Well, Theodosia, you must brave yourself for the infliction.

(*Enter* Mrs. Stuart Bidderby *and* Miss Dexter.)

Dear child, how glad I am to see you! And — (*Pausing and looking at* Miss Dexter.)

MRS. BIDDERBY. My friend, Miss Dexter, who is visiting me for a week.

MRS. T. Miss Dexter, I am delighted. (*To* MRS. BIDDERBY.) So kind of you to give me this pleasure. (*Seats* MISS DEXTER *by pile of photographs, and draws* MRS. BIDDERBY *down beside her.*) I suppose you have been in New York before, Miss Dexter?

MISS D. Oh, yes; quite often.

MRS. T. No need to ask if you like New York; every one does, you know.

MISS D. No — (*quickly correcting herself*) — I mean, yes — yes; of course I like New York. (*Falls to examining photographs.*)

MRS. B. (*in a low tone to* MRS. TAXTON). Engaged! A bit absent-minded, you know. He isn't here.

MRS. T. Oh! (*Looks at* MISS DEXTER.) That reminds me. What do you think I've just heard from that precious cousin of mine?

MRS. B. Frederick the Great?

MRS. T. Yes.

MRS. B. Is it startling?

MRS. T. Well, rather.

MRS. B. Then it can't be that he's engaged; that happens too often to him to be anything out of the common. (*At the word "engaged"* MISS DEXTER *looks up, becomes interested, but goes on looking at the photographs.*)

MRS. T. Oh, now, you're not quite fair to Fred. I know he flirts —

MRS. B. Flirts? Good heavens! That's no name for it. He used to propose to a girl on an average of once a month right along. Perhaps he has reformed, now that he's gone in for the right thing.

MRS. T. Oh, I assure you he is frightfully in earnest this time!

MRS. B. Now, what sort of a woman do you imagine

he's going to marry? Large, black-eyed girl, don't you think?

MRS. T. Oh, yes; a regular Juno. He always admired tall women.

MISS D. (*looks down on her small proportions a trifle depreciatingly, then smiles and murmurs aside*). I'm glad my dear boy doesn't. I'm glad he likes small girls.

MRS. T. She has masses of dark hair, looks well in diamonds, and delights in wearing yellow. Fred always wanted the sort of woman who could make a show at the head of his table, and whom he could exhibit to the boys. He always said sweet, unsophisticated innocence was all very well in looks, but his wife should be a woman of the world.

MISS D. (*aside*). That's so different from my Fred.

MRS. B. But now, really; do you think Fred is capable of loving any woman very long at a time?

MRS. T. Indeed, I do! If he has made up his mind to be married — if it has really come down to that, you know — and he is determined to give up his bachelor apartments, club nights, suppers, and all that sort of thing, he must be very much in love, more than he's ever been before.

MRS. B. Did he send you a picture of his Juno, his goddess, etc.?

MRS. T. No; I'll see that when he arrives, I suppose. By the way, here's a recent one of his he sent me last week. (*Rises and goes to desk, gets photograph, and brings it to* MRS. BIDDERBY.)

MRS. B. (*looking at picture*). He looks well. Being engaged seems to agree with him. He seems actually happy.

MISS D. (*smiling*). I'm getting interested in that engaged man. Can I see his picture?

MRS. T. Certainly, Miss Dexter. Agnes, pass it along when you get through gazing on his happiness.

MRS. B. (*with mock sadness*). Alas! poor Yorick! He that was wont to set the table in a roar. Take him, dear.

The sight saddens me. (*Hands photograph to* MISS DEXTER, *and crosses over to table for cup of tea;* MRS. TAXTON *pours for her.*)

MISS D. (*takes photograph, looks, starts, turns very pale, but tries to control herself. Speaks brokenly, aside*). My Fred! (*Looks at photograph with eyes that seem to burn through it, when* MRS. BIDDERBY *turns and notices her.*)

MRS. B. Why, dear, you look as if you might have been one of Fred's numerous victims.

MISS D. (*forcing a smile*). Do I? (*Aside.*) It seems I am. (*Drops photographs, rises, goes to window, and looks out.*)

MRS. T. Miss Dexter, I'm afraid we've been boring you horribly. You must forgive two old friends when they get together, talking over family matters. I'm sure our chatter must have been anything but interesting to you.

MISS D. (*turning from window to look at a picture*). Oh, but it was — it's very interesting to me.

MRS. T. Well, now, we'll try to make amends by talking about something else. Have you seen —

MISS D. (*quickly*). The gentleman's name is Towers, is it not? Mr. Fred Towers?

MRS. T. Yes.

MRS. B. (*jokingly*). I thought you'd been one of his victims.

MRS. T. Then you know him, Miss Dexter?

MISS D. Yes, I've met him. Did he tell you in the letter the — the lady's name? (*Clutches her hands tightly together, and bites her lips, as, with face turned away from the others, she tries to control her feelings.*)

MRS. T. No; not unless he hid it away in one corner, where I didn't look. I hadn't quite finished reading it when you came in. I'll see. (*Gets up and looks for letter.*)

MISS D. (*trying to force a laugh*). But you're sure she's a tall brunette, who loves yellow, has black eyes, and wears diamonds? A striking sort of woman one he'd like to show, his friends?

MRS. T. (*still searching*). I think so — I don't know. (*Impatiently.*) What did I do with that letter?

MISS D. (*aside*). My God! Shall I get through this without letting them know?

MRS. B. Oh, never mind hunting any more, Docie; it doesn't matter.

MISS D. (*quickly*). Yes it — I mean — I'll — I'll help you if you wish. I really want to know (*forces a laugh*) about this mysterious woman. (*Turns and staggers slightly, catches at chair.*)

MRS. B. Sit down, dear, and let me give you a cup of tea while Mrs. Taxton is looking. (*Seeing her face.*) Why, aren't you well?

MISS D. Oh, yes; perfectly.

MRS. B. You'll have some tea?

MISS D. (*sinking weakly in chair*). No — no, I thank you.

MRS. T. (*lifting up a book, and finding letter*). Well, there! Did you ever see anything like that? Some inanimate things, like this letter, actually seem alive, and to take a fiendish delight in creating a disturbance. (*Looking at it.*) Oh, here's a lot on the other side I didn't see. (*Scanning page.*) Gushing over her in the most absurd way. Will he never come to the name. Oh! (*Reading.*) "I call her Violet, because she has eyes like those dear single little blossoms we used to find in the woods. That isn't her real name, though. It's quite a stately one. Her given names are Gertrude Volney" — (MISS DEXTER *suddenly gives an ecstatic little* "Oh!" *and quietly faints away.*)

MRS. B. (*seeing her*). Docie! Quick! Some wine! Brandy! Smelling-salts! Good Lord! She's the one!

SCENE FROM THE "SCOTTISH CHIEFS."

BY JANE PORTER.

CHARACTERS.

HELEN MAR.
LADY RUTHVEN, *her aunt.*

HELEN MAR (*contemplating a portrait of* WILLIAM WALLACE). There are the lofty meditations of a royal mind, devising the freedom of his people. Ah! how blest Scotland must be under his reign! Were this a canonized saint, how gladly would I fall down and worship him. Yes, though I were a peasant girl, and he did not know that Helen Mar ever existed. That I could be near him and wait on his smiles! But that may not be; I am a woman, and formed to suffer in silence and seclusion. But even at a distance, brave Wallace, my spirit shall watch over you, and my prayers shall follow you, so that when we meet in heaven, the Blessed Virgin shall say that through my vigils her angels have surrounded thee — (*Noise without.*) He must be near; he whose smile is more precious to me than the adulation of all the world beside, now smiles upon every one! All look upon him, all hear him, but I — and I — Ah, Wallace, did thy dead wife Marion love thee dearer?

(*Enter* LADY RUTHVEN *hurriedly.*)

LADY RUTHVEN. Helen, I would not disturb you before; but as *you* were to be absent, *I* would not make one of Lady Mar's train; and I come to enjoy with you the return

59

of our beloved regent. (*She takes* HELEN'S *hand, and tries to draw her to the window.* HELEN *shrinks back.*)

HELEN. I hear enough, dear aunt; sights like these overcome me: let me remain where I am.

LADY R. (*running to window*). He comes, Helen; he comes! Oh! how princely he looks! They shower flowers upon him from the houses, and how sweetly he smiles. Come, Helen, come, if you would see the perfection of majesty and modesty united in one. (*Goes back to* HELEN *and sits down by her.*) Depend upon it, my child, before he was Lady Marion's husband, he must have heard sighs enough from the fairest in the land to have turned the wits of half the male world. And, methinks, the gentlest lady would be excused for leaving hall and bower to follow him. But, alas! he is now for none on earth. That a man so noble — so fond a husband — should be deprived of the wife on whom he doted — that, when he shall die, nothing will be left of William Wallace — breaks my heart.

HELEN (*who has been very agitated during* LADY RUTHVEN'S *speech, raises her head with animation*). Ah, my aunt, will he not leave behind him the liberty of Scotland? That is an offspring worthy of his god-like soul.

LADY R. True, my child. But — here comes our deliverer again. It will do you good, as it did me, to look on his beneficent face. (*Draws* HELEN *to window.*)

HELEN. Ah, it is he indeed! No dream, no illusion, but his very self. (*Turns away from window, and throws herself weeping in* LADY RUTHVEN'S *arms.*)

LADY R. There, my child, be comforted. Wallace cannot always be insensible to so much excellence.

HELEN. My more than mother, fear me not! I am grateful to Sir William Wallace. I venerate him as the Southrons do St. George; but I need not your tender pity. (*Forces a smile.*)

LADY R. My sweetest Helen, how can I pity her for whom I hope everything.

SCENE FROM THE "SCOTTISH CHIEFS." 61

HELEN. Hope nothing for me; but to see me a vestal here and a saint in heaven.

LADY R. What say you? Who would talk of being a vestal with such a heart in view as that of the regent of Scotland? and that it will be yours, does not his eloquent gratitude declare.

HELEN (*casting her eyes down*). No, my aunt; gratitude is eloquent where love would be silent. I am not so sacrilegious as to wish that Sir William Wallace should transfer that heart to me, which the blood of Marion forever purchased.

LADY R. Gentlest of human beings! Whatever be thy lot, it must be happy.

HELEN. Whatever it be, I know there is an Almighty reason for it.

LADY R. Oh! that the ears of Wallace could hear thee!

HELEN. They will some time, dear aunt.

LADY R. When, where, dearest? (HELEN *points to heaven;* LADY RUTHVEN *gazes at her a moment in speechless admiration, then draws her to her and kisses her.*) Blame me not, Helen, that I forget probability in grasping at a possibility which might give me such a nephew as Sir William Wallace, and you a husband worthy of your merits.

HELEN. No more of this, if you love me, dear aunt. It neither can nor ought to be. So, no more.

THE SUPPLICATION.

(From " Unknown to History.")

BY CHARLOTTE M. YONGE.

CHARACTERS.

QUEEN ELIZABETH.
CICELY TALBOT.
RICHARD TALBOT, *her adopted father.*

QUEEN ELIZABETH (*seated alone in an arm-chair by a table. Enter* CICELY *and* RICHARD). How now, whom have you brought hither, Monsieur?

CICELY (*kneeling*). It is I, so please your Majesty, I, who have come hither to lay before your Majesty a letter from my mother, the Queen of Scots.

(ELIZABETH *utters an incredulous exclamation of surprise.*)

CIC. If it will please your Majesty to look at this letter, you will see the proofs of what I say, and that I am indeed Bride Hepburn, the daughter of Queen Mary's last marriage. (*Rising.*) I was born at Lochleven on the 20th of February, of the year of grace, 1567, and thence secretly sent in the "Bride of Dunbar" to be bred up in France. The ship was wrecked, and all were lost; but I was, by the grace of God, picked up by a good and gallant gentleman, Master Richard Talbot, who brought me up as his own daughter, all unknowing whence I came or who I was, until three years ago, when one of the secret agents made known to the Queen of Scots that I was the babe who had been embarked in the "Bride of Dunbar." I have always borne the name Cicely Talbot, and but few know my real birth.

Eliz. Verily, thou must be a bold wench to expect me to believe such a mere minstrel's tale.

Cic. Nevertheless, madam, it is the simple truth, as you will see if you deign to open this packet.

Eliz. And who or where is this same honorable gentleman who brought you up — Richard Talbot?

Cic. He is here, madam. He will confirm all I say.

Eliz. Master Talbot, how is this? You, that have been vaunted to us as the very pink of fidelity, working up a tale that smacks mightily of treason and leasing.

Richard. The truth is often stranger than any playwright can devise.

Eliz. If it be truth, the worse for you, sir. What color can you give to thus hiding one who might, forsooth, claim royal blood, tainted though it be?

Rich. Pardon me, your Grace. For many years I knew not who the babe was whom I had taken from the wreck, and when the secret of her birth was discovered, I deemed it not mine own, but that of the Queen of Scots.

Eliz. A captive's secrets are not her own, and are only kept by traitors.

Cic. Madam, madam, traitor never was named in the same breath with Master Talbot's name. If he kept the secret, it was out of pity, and knowing no hurt could come to your Majesty by it.

Eliz. Thou hast a tongue, wench, be thou who thou mayst. This must be further inquired into.

Cic. Madam! it will not matter. No trouble shall ever be caused by my drop of royal blood. I seek not state; all I ask is my mother's life. O madam, would you but see her and speak with her, you would know how far from her thoughts is any evil to your royal person.

Eliz. Tush, wench! we know better. Is this thy lesson?

CIC. None hath taught me any lesson, madam. I know what my mother's enemies have, as they say, proved against her, and I know they say that while she lives your Grace cannot be in security.

ELIZ. That is what moves my people to demand her death.

CIC. It is not of your own free will, madam, nor of your own kind heart; that I well know. And, madam, I will show you a way. Let but my mother be escorted to some convent abroad, in France or Austria, and her name should be hidden from every one. None would know where to find her, and she would leave in your hands and those of the Parliament, a resignation of all of her claims.

ELIZ. And who is to answer that, when once beyond English bounds, she should not stir up more trouble than ever?

CIC. That do I. Here am I, Bride Hepburn, ready to live in your Majesty's hands as a hostage, whom you might put to death at the first stirring on her behalf.

ELIZ. Foolish maid! thou mayst purpose as thou sayst, but I know what wenches are made of too well to' trust thee.

CIC. Ah, madam, pardon me, but you know not how strong a maiden's heart can be for a mother's sake. Madam! you have never seen my mother. If you but knew her patience and tenderness, you would know how not I, but every man or woman in her train, would gladly lay down life and liberty for her.

ELIZ. Strange, strange matters, and they need to be duly considered.

CIC. I will then abide your Majesty's pleasure, craving license that it may be at Fotheringay with my mother.

ELIZ. And would she do this? Am I to take it on thy word, girl?

CIC. Your Majesty knows this ring sent to her at Lochleven. It is the pledge that she binds herself to these conditions. May I carry the tidings to her? I can go with this gentleman as Cis Talbot returning to her service. (ELIZABETH *bends her head as though assenting;* CICELY *clasping her hands delightedly.*) How shall I thank you, gracious Queen?

ELIZ. (*cutting her short*). What means the wench? I have promised nothing. I have only said I will look into this strange story of thine, and consider this proposal — that is, if thy mother, as thou callest her, truly intends it — ay, and will keep to it.

CIC. That is all I could ask of your Majesty. The next messenger after my return shall carry her full consent to these conditions, and there will I abide your pleasure until the time come for her to be conducted to her convent. O madam, I see mercy in your looks. Receive a daughter's blessing and thanks!

ELIZ. Over fast, over fast, maiden! Who told thee that I had consented?

CIC. Your Majesty's own countenance. I see pity in it, and the recollection that all posterity for evermore will speak of the clemency of Elizabeth as the crown of all her glories.

MOTHER AND CHILD.

(From " Unknown to History.")

BY CHARLOTTE M. YONGE.

CHARACTERS.

MARY QUEEN OF SCOTS.
CICELY TALBOT.

(The scene is laid in a room in the castle of Sheffield during the time of captivity of MARY QUEEN OF SCOTS. *The* QUEEN *is seated in a despondent attitude, but brightens as she sees* CICELY TALBOT *approach.)*

MARY. Thou art come forth once more to rejoice mine eyes, a sight for sair een, as they say in Scotland. (CICELY *kneels, and kisses her extended hand;* MARY *raises her, and kisses her cheek.)* Little one, I would fain have thee stay with me. Wilt thou stoop to come and cheer the poor old caged bird?

CICELY. O madam, how gladly will I do so if I may!

MAR. Welcome, then, my sweet little Scot — one more loyal subject come to me in bondage. And now, let me see the poor little shoulder that hath suffered so much. How is the hurt?

CIC. My arm is still bound, madam.

MAR. *(turning back her sleeve and exclaiming).* There! sooth enough! Monsieur Gorian could swear to them instantly.

CIC. What is it? Oh, what is it, madam? Is there anything on my arm? No plague spot, I hope.

MAR. (*laughing*). No plague spot, sweet one, save, perhaps, in the eyes of you Protestants; but to me they are a gladsome sight — a token I never hoped to see. (*Kisses the arm.*) And so, she thought she had the plague spot on her little white shoulder. Did'st thou really not know what marks thou bearest, little one?

CIC. No, madam.

MAR. Listen, child! (*Sitting down.*) Give me thine hand, and I will tell thee a tale. There was a lonely castle in a lake, grim, cold and northernly; and thither there was brought, by angry men, a captive woman. They had dealt with her strangely and subtilly; they had laid on her the guilt of the crimes themselves had wrought, and when she clung to the one man whom she thought honest, they forced her into wedding, only that all the world might cry out upon her, forsake her, and deliver her up into those cruel hands. Thou dost pity that poor lady, sweet one? There was little pity for her then! She had looked her last on her lad-bairn; ay, and they had said she had striven to poison him, and they were breeding him up to loathe the very name of his mother. And so it was, that the lady vowed, if another babe was granted to her, these foes of hers should have no knowledge of its existence, but it should be bred up beyond their ken. The poor mother durst have scarce one hour's joy of her first and only daughter ere the trusty Gorian took the little one from her. Not one more embrace could I be granted, but my good chaplain baptized her in secret, and Gorian set two marks on the soft flesh, which he said never could be blotted out, and undertook to carry her to France, with a letter of mine bound up in her swathing clothes, committing her to the charge of my good aunt, the Abbess of Soissons, in utter secrecy, until better days should come. Alas! I thought them not so far off. Long, long did I hope that my little one was safely sheltered in the dear old cloister; but at length I heard that the ship in which she sailed, the "Bride of Dunbar," had never been heard of more. And I — I shed some tears, but I could not grieve that that child of sorrow was cradled in Paradise.

CIC. (*after a pause, in a trembling voice*).   And it was from the wreck of the "Bride of Dunbar" that I was taken.

MAR.   Thou hast said it, child!   (*Embracing her.*)   My bairn, my bonnie bairn!   Speak to me!   Let me hear my child's voice.

CIC.   Oh, madam —

MAR.   Call me mother!   Never have I heard that sound from my child's lips.   Speak, child — let me hear thee.

CIC.   Mother, my mother — Pardon me, I know not — I cannot say what I would.   But oh!   I would do anything for — for — your Grace.

MAR.   There, there!   I ask thee not to share my sorrows and my woes.   That, Heaven forbid!   I ask thee but to come from time to time to cheer me, and lie on my wearing bosom to still its yearning, and let me feel that I have indeed a child.   Be Cicely Talbot by day as ever — only at night be mine — my child, my Bride, for so wast thou named after our Scottish patroness.   It was her ship in which thou didst sail; and lo, she guarded thee, and not merely saved thee from death, but provided thee a happy and joyous home.   We must render her thanks, my child.

CIC.   In sooth, madam, it seems that I am two maidens in one — Cis Talbot by day, and Bride of Scotland by night.

MAR.   That is well.   We must hold our peace and keep our counsel.   Remember that did the bruit once get abroad, thou wouldst assuredly be torn from me, to be mewed up by the English Queen.   But cheer up, lassie, better days are coming.   Our faithful lieges shall soon open the way to freedom and royalty; and I pray the saints that thy days may be happier and more enduring than ever were mine.

A REVELATION.

(*Scene from " Romola."*)

BY GEORGE ELIOT.

CHARACTERS.

ROMOLA.
TITO.

(*It is dusk.* ROMOLA *enters the library, lights the lamp, and begins her work, copying the catalogue. To her surprise* TITO *enters. She runs towards him.*)

ROMOLA. Tito, dearest, I did not know you would come so soon.

TITO (*smiling, and putting his arm around her*). I am not welcome, then?

ROM. (*reproachfully*). Tito! (*Helping him take off his wraps.*) If I had expected you so soon, I would have had a little festival prepared to this joyful ringing of the bells. I did not mean to be here in the library when you came home.

TITO. Never mind, sweet. Do not think about the fire. Come — come and sit down. (*He sits in a chair, and she on a low stool beside him, resting one arm on his knee.*)

ROM. I have been enjoying the clang of the bells for the first time, Tito. I liked being shaken and deafened by them. I fancied I was something like a Bacchante possessed by a divine rage. Are not the people looking very joyful to-night?

69

Tito. Joyful after a sour and pious fashion. But in truth, those who are left behind have little cause to be joyful; it seems to me the most reasonable ground of gladness would be to have got out of Florence.

Rom. Why, Tito? Are there any fresh troubles?

Tito. No need of fresh ones, Romola. There are three strong parties in the city, all ready to fly at each other's throats. For my part, I have been thinking seriously that we should be wise to quit Florence, my Romola.

Rom. (*starting*). Tito, how could we leave Florence? Surely you do not think I could leave it — at least, not yet — not for a long time.

Tito. That is all a fabric of your own imagination, my sweet one. Your secluded life has made you lay such false stress on a few things. I like people who take life less eagerly; and it would be good for my Romola too, to see a new life. I should like to dip her a little in the soft waters of forgetfulness. (*He leans forward and kisses her brow; but she does not notice it.*)

Rom. Tito, it is not because I suppose Florence is the pleasantest place in the world that I desire not to quit it It is because I — because we have to see my father's wish fulfilled. My godfather is old — he is seventy-one — we could not leave him to undertake it.

Tito. It is precisely those superstitions which hang about you, that make me obliged to take care of you in opposition to your will. You know, dearest — your own clear judgment always showed you — that the notion of isolating a collection of books and antiquities, and attaching a single name to them forever, was one that had no valid, substantial good for its object. I understand your feeling about the wishes of the dead, but you gave your life to your father while he lived; why should you demand more of yourself?

Rom. Because it was a trust. He trusted me; he trusted

you, Tito. I did not expect you to feel anything else about it — to feel as I do — but I did expect you to feel that.

TITO. Yes, dearest, of course I should feel it on a point where your father's real welfare or happiness were concerned; but there is no question of that now. Ask yourself what good can these books do stored together under your father's name in Florence, more than they would do if they were divided or carried elsewhere?

ROM. (*drawing away her arm from his knee, and sitting motionless with her arms clasped before her*). You talk of substantial good, Tito? Are faithfulness and love and sweet, grateful memories no good? Is it no good that a just life should be justly honored? I would give up anything else, Tito — I would leave Florence — what else did I live for but for him and you? But I will not give up that duty. It was a yearning of his heart, and therefore a yearning of mine.

TITO. I am sorry to hear you speak in that spirit of blind persistence, my Romola, because it obliges me to give you pain. But I partly foresaw your opposition, and, as a prompt decision was necessary, I avoided that obstacle, and decided without consulting you. The very care of a husband for his wife's interest compels him to that separate action sometimes — even when he has such a wife as you, my Romola. (*She turns her eyes on him in breathless inquiry.*) I mean that I have arranged for the transfer, both of books and antiquities, where they will find the highest use and value.

ROM. (*starting from her seat*). You have *sold* them?

TITO. I have. The books have been bought for the Duke of Milan; the marbles and bronzes and the rest are going to France, and both will be protected by the stability of a great Power, instead of remaining in a city which is exposed to ruin.

ROM. You are a treacherous man! (*Turning away.*) It may be hindered — I am going to my godfather.

TITO (*locks door and takes key out*). Try to calm yourself a little, Romola. It is of no use for you to go to your god-father. Messer Bernardo cannot reverse what I have done. Only sit down. You would hardly wish, if you were quite yourself, to make known to any third person what passes between us in private.

ROM. Why can it not be reversed? Nothing is moved yet.

TITO. Simply because the sale has been concluded by written agreement, the purchasers have left Florence, and I hold the bonds for the purchase-money.

ROM. If my father had suspected you of being a faith-less man, he would have placed the library safely out of your power. But death overtook him too soon, and when you were sure his ear was deaf and his hand stiff, you robbed him. Have you robbed somebody else who is *not* dead? Is that the reason you wear armor?

TITO. It is useless to answer the words of madness, Romola. The event is irrevocable, the library is sold, and you are my wife.

ROM. (*remaining silent, and looking on the ground for some time*). I have one thing to ask.

TITO. Ask anything that I can do without injuring us both, Romola.

ROM. That you will give me that portion of the money that belongs to my godfather, and let me pay him.

TITO. I must have some assurance from you, first, of the attitude you intend to take towards me.

ROM. Do you believe in assurances, Tito? (*Bitterly.*)

TITO. From you, I do.

ROM. I will do you no harm. I will disclose nothing. You say truly, the event is irrevocable.

TITO. Then I will do what you desire to-morrow morning.

ROM. To-night, if possible, that we may not speak of it again.

TITO. It is possible. (*He goes to other side of room, and* ROMOLA *sits down. Presently he comes back and puts a piece of paper in her hand.*) You will receive something in return, you are aware, my Romola?

ROM. (*taking paper, but not looking up*). Yes, I understand.

TITO. And you will forgive me, my Romola, when you have had time to reflect.

(*He touches her brow with his lips, unlocks the door, and goes out.* ROMOLA *moves her head and listens. The great door of the court is opened and shut. She starts up as if some sudden freedom had come, and going to her father's chair, where his picture is propped, falls on her knees before it, and bursts into sobs.*

A COQUETTE IN DIFFICULTIES.

PY RHODA BROUGHTON.

CHARACTERS.

BELINDA, *a proper young woman.*
SARAH, *sister to* BELINDA.

(BELINDA *seated, reading; enter* SARAH.)

SARAH. Are you alone?

BEL. (*crossly*). Of course I am alone. Am I in the habit of receiving in my bedroom?

SAR. The moment is apparently not a propitious one, but as my need is sore, I am afraid I cannot afford to wait for a better. I have come, my Belinda, to ask a favor of you.

BEL. Then you may go away again at once, for I tell you once for all, I will not grant it.

SAR. What! refuse even before you hear what it is?

BEL. Do you think I do not recognize that well-known formula? I am sure that I have heard it often enough. It means that you expect me to tell Professor Forth that you have every intention of jilting him!

SAR. You word it coarsely, but I have heard worse guesses.

BEL. Then I absolutely and flatly refuse the office! *Why* you engaged yourself to him in the first instance—

SAR. *Why*, indeed? You may well ask!

BEL. And yet, when you wrote to announce your engagement to me, you said that you did not know what you had done to deserve such happiness!

74

SAR. I did not — I did not. (*Putting hands before face.*) It is not true. It was not about him; it was one of the others.

BEL. (*scornfully.*) *One of the others!* How pleasant and dignified to be bandied about! *One of the others!*

SAR. It may not be dignified, but it is not so very unpleasant!

BEL. You know that I took a solemn oath to wash my hands of your affairs, last time, when I had that painful scene with poor young Manners, and he walked round the room on his knees after me, clutching my skirts and sobbing!

SAR. (*hard-heartedly*). He always sobbed! I have seen him cry like a pump!

BEL. I have already told six men that you had only been making fools of them.

SAR. Six! Come now, gently.

BEL. I repeat, six! In fact, I think I am rather understating it; and I *will not* tell a seventh.

SAR. A seventh!!!

BEL. If you imply that I am exaggerating, I am quite willing to count. First (*checking off on her fingers*), young Manners!

SAR. We have had him once already.

BEL. Second, Colonel Green. Poor fellow! he sobbed too!

SAR. More shame for him. (*Brazenly.*)

BEL. Third — the young clergyman whom you picked up at the seaside, and whose name I can never remember.

SAR. (*with animation*). No more can I! How strange! Pooh! What was it again? Did it begin with a B?

BEL. Fourth — old Lord Blucher, who was so deaf that I could not get him to understand what I meant.

SAR. (*thoughtfully*). I am almost sure that it began with an L.

BEL. Fifth — Mr. Brabazon.

SAR.   You counted him before.

BEL.   I did not!

SAR.   I think you did.

BEL.   I am sure I did not; but to make certain, we will begin all over again.   First — poor young Manners —

SAR.   (*putting fingers in ears; gets up*).   Stop!   I will grant that there were six, sixteen, sixty — anything to put an end to that intolerable arithmetic of yours.

BEL.   What could have been your inducement in this case?   I am quite at a loss to conjecture; it certainly could have been neither pleasure nor profit.

SAR.   It certainly could not.   (*Sighing.*)   Any one who saw him would exonerate me from the suspicion of either motive.

BEL.   Such a conquest could not have even gratified your vanity.

SAR. (*animatedly*).   Yes, but it did!   *You* may not think much of him, but I can assure you that he is considered a great luminary at Oxbridge.   At the house where I met him they could not make enough of him; it seems he has written a book upon the Digamma!

BEL.   And what is the Digamma?

SAR.   You do not know what the Digamma is?   Well, then (*laughing*), to tell you a secret, no more do I!

BEL. (*grimly*).   You cannot live upon the Digamma, I suppose!

SAR. (*still laughing*).   I should be sorry to try.

BEL.   Then I am quite as much in the dark as ever!

SAR. (*sits down*).   Well, it was not *only* the Digamma, of course, though as far as I could make out, that appeared to be the principal thing, but he was looked upon as a genius generally.   You should have seen how they all sat at his feet — such feet! — and hung on his words.   There was one girl who waited on him hand and foot.   She always warmed his great-coat for him, and helped him on with his galoches.

BEL.   Well?

SAR.   Well, you know (*impatiently*), one would not have been human if one could have stood calmly by and looked on. I rushed into the fray; I too warmed his great-coat and put on his galoches! Ugh! what a size they were! I could have lived roomily and commodiously in one of them!

BEL.   Well?

SAR.   *Well*, indeed! I do not call it at all well! I call it very ill!

BEL.   There I have the good fortune thoroughly to agree with you.

SAR.   Well, as I was saying (*sighing heavily*), I rushed into the fray. I was successful, dreadfully successful! You know the sequel, as they say in books.

BEL. (*sternly*). I do not know the sequel; all I know is that I will have neither part nor lot in it!

SAR.   No? and yet (*fawningly*) it would come so much better from you.

BEL.   Better or worse, it will not come from me.

SAR.   When *you* break it to them (*sidling up*), it does not hurt them nearly so much! I declare, I think they almost like it!

BEL. (*after a moment's silence*). Why, at least, did you drag him here?

SAR. (*hanging her head*). I am afraid I cannot quite defend it; but to tell the truth — which indeed I always try to do — times were slack! There was nobody else much just then, and I thought I could at least make him fetch and carry! I was grossly deceived; he is too disobliging to fetch, and too much afraid of over-fatiguing himself to carry. Now, if the cases were reversed (*going up to her*), if *you* were in difficulties —

BEL.   I never am in difficulties.

SAR.   I do not see much to brag of in that, for my part! (*Sitting down.*)

BEL. (*dryly*). No more do I. I am never in difficulties, as you call them, because I never have any temptation to be ! Perhaps if I had I might; but, as you are well aware (*sighing*), I have not, and never had, any charm for men

SAR. It is very odd, is it not? I cannot think why it is. I have often wondered what the reason could be ; sometimes I think it is your nose !

BEL. (*putting up her hand*). My nose? What is the matter with my nose ?

SAR. There is nothing the matter with it; perhaps it would be better for you if there were: it is only too good! I cannot fancy any man venturing to love such a nose; it looks too high and mighty to inspire anything short of veneration !

BEL. It is not so *very* high, either ! (*Measuring with handkerchief.*) There ! only that much.

SAR. (*gravely*). It is not a case of measurement; I have seen noses several hands higher that were not nearly so alarming. It is a case of feeling; somehow yours makes them feel small. Take my word for it (*shrewdly*), the one thing that they never can either forgive or forget is to be made to feel small.

BEL. It is clear, then, that nothing short of amputation could make me attractive, and I am afraid even that might fail; but I do not know why we digressed to me at all.

SAR. I had a little plan (*gloomily*), but you have frightened it away.

BEL. (*shortly*). What is it?

SAR. (*kneeling*). Well, you know that we are going to drive to Moritzburg to-day, you and I. Of course Professor Forth (*grimacing*) will be on duty there to meet us; equally of course young Rivers (BELINDA *starts*), who seems to have contracted a not altogether reprehensible habit of dogging our steps, will be there too.

BEL. (*averting her face*). Well ?

SAR. Well, I thought — but you are not a pleasant person to unfold one's little schemes to — I thought that for once you might be obliging, and pair off casually with my dear, and take an opportunity of softly breathing to him that nobody — I least of all — will try to stop him if he effects a graceful retreat to Oxbridge and the Digamma !

BEL. (*low, suppressed voice*). And meanwhile you ?

SAR. (*jovially*). And meanwhile I (*getting up*), killing two birds with one stone, shall be straying hand in hand through the vernal woods with —

BEL. (*rising abruptly*). I have already told you that I utterly decline to be mixed up in your entanglements. I forbid you to mention the subject to me again.

SAR. (*sitting down*). Whew-w-w-w ! Forbid ! what an ugly word ! After all, I am not much surprised that men are frightened at you. I am frightened at you myself sometimes, and so no wonder that they shake in their shoes, and dare not call their harmless souls their own.

BEL. (*turning on* SARAH). How many times are you going to tell me that ? Do you think that it can be very pleasant to hear that I can never inspire anything but alarm and aversion ? I am as well aware of it as you can be ; but I am a little tired of hearing it. (*Exit.*)

SAR. And you might inspire such different feelings ; it *is* a pity to see advantages which would have made me famous if I had had them, absolutely thrown away upon you ! I suppose (*sighing*) that it is the old story of the people with large appetites and nothing to eat, and the people with plenty to eat and no appetites.

THE CHILD-ANGEL AND HER WOES.

By James De Mille.

CHARACTERS.

Minnie, *the Child-Angel.*
Kitty, *her married sister.*

(Minnie, *reading; enter* Kitty, *and throws her arms around her.*)

Minnie. Kitty!

Kitty. O Minnie, my poor darling! what is all this about Vesuvius? Is it true? I will never dare to leave you again. As to Ethel, I am astonished. She is the very last person I would have supposed capable of leading you into danger.

Min. Now, Kitty dearest, that's not true; she didn't lead me at all. I led her.

Kit. And did you really get into the crater?

Min. Oh, I suppose so! They all said so. (*Folding her hands.*) I only remember some smoke, and then jolting about dreadfully on the shoulder of some great — big — awful — man.

Kit. (*sighing*). Oh, dear!

Min. What's the matter, Kitty dearest?

Kit. Another man!

Min. Well, how *could* I help it? I'm *sure* I didn't want him. I don't see *why* they all act so. If people *will* go and save my life, I can't help it. I think it's very, very horrid of them!

Kit. Oh, dear! oh, dear!

(*Reprinted by permission of Harper and Brothers.*)

MIN. Now, Kitty, stop!

KIT. Another man!

MIN. If you are so unkind, I'll cry. You're always teasing me. You know I want comfort, and I'm not strong; and I really think I'd rather not live at all if my life *has* to be saved so often. I'm sure I never heard of any person who is always going and getting her life saved, and bothered and proposed to and written to and frightened to death.

KIT. Really now, Minnie, you must remember that you are in a serious position. There is that wretched Captain Kirby.

MIN. (*sighing*). I know.

KIT. He thinks that you are engaged to him. And that dreadful American. And then there is that pertinacious Count Girasole. Think what trouble we had in getting rid of him. And I know he will come upon us again somewhere, and we'll have all the trouble over again.

MIN. Well, I can't hurt their feelings when they've saved my life.

KIT. Well, but, darling, how did this happen?

MIN. Oh, don't, don't! It's too horrible!

KIT. Poor darling — the crater?

MIN. No; the great, big man. I didn't see any crater.

KIT. Weren't you in the crater?

MIN. No, I wasn't.

KIT. They said you were.

MIN. I wasn't. I was on the back of a big, horrid man, who gave great jumps down the side of an awful mountain, and threw me down at the bottom of it, and — and — disarranged all my hair. And I was so frightened that I couldn't even cur — cur — cry. (*Sobbing.*)

KIT. (*petting her*). No-o-o-o, nun-no-o-o, darling.

MIN. The next time I lose my life, I don't want to be saved — I want them to let me alone, and I'll come home myself.

KIT. So you shall, darling; you shall do just as you please.

MIN. Well, then, I want you to tell me what I am to do.

KIT. About what?

MIN. Why, about this great, big, horrid man.

KIT. Very well. Tell me first how you happened to get into such danger.

MIN. Well, you know we went for a drive, and we drove along for miles. When all at once I saw a gentleman on horseback, oh, *so* handsome!—and he was looking at poor little me as though he would eat me up. And the moment I saw him I was frightened out of my poor little wits, for I knew he was coming to save my life.

KIT. You poor little puss! what put such an idea in your ridiculous little head?

MIN. I knew it; second sight, you know. So I sat looking at him, and I whispered to myself all the time, "Oh, please don't! ple-e-e-ease let me alone! I don't want to be saved at all!" And the more I said it, the more he seemed to fix his eyes upon me.

KIT. It was very rude of him, I think.

MIN. (*sharply*). It wasn't rude at all. He pretended to be looking at the sea, but all the time he saw me out of the corner of his eye, — this way.

KIT. He didn't look at you that way, I hope.

MIN. There is nothing to laugh at. He looked awfully solemn. Well, at last we got to Vesuvius, and he came too, and I teased Ethel to go to the cone. The men took us up on chairs, and all the time the stranger was in sight. He walked up by himself, with great, big, long, strong strides. When we got to the top I was dying with curiosity to look down and see where the smoke came from. The stranger was standing there too, and that's what made me excited. (KITTY *shudders and takes her hand.*) There was no end of smoke, and it was awfully unpleasant, and I suddenly

fainted. Well, now, the very — next — thing — I remember
is this, and it's horrible. I felt awful jolts, and found myself in the arms of a big, horrid man, who was running down
the side of the mountain with dreadfully long jumps. At
last he laid me down. And O Kitty darling, you have no
idea what I suffered! He was rubbing my hands, and sighing and groaning. I stole a little bit of a look at him —
just a little bit of a bit — and saw tears in his eyes. I knew
he was going to propose on the spot, and shut my eyes
tighter than ever.

KIT. Well?

MIN. Well, at last I spoke as low as I could, and asked,
"Is that you, papa dear?"

KIT. Well?

MIN. Well —

KIT. Well, go on.

MIN. Well, he said — he said, "Yes, darling" — and —

KIT. And what?

MIN. And he kissed me.

KIT. Kissed you?

MIN. Y — yes, and I think it's a shame.

KIT. The miserable wretch!

MIN. No, he isn't. He isn't a miserable wretch at all.
He only pretended.

KIT. Pretended what?

MIN. Why, that he was my — my father, you know.

KIT. I'll tell him what I think of him.

MIN. But he saved my life, and you know you can't be
very harsh with him. Please don't — pl-e-e-ease, now!

KIT. Why, you don't want another man, I hope?

MIN. N-no; but then I don't want to hurt his feelings.

KIT. Do you know the name of this last one?

MIN. Oh, yes.

KIT. What is it?

MIN. It's a funny name. Scone Dacres.

KIT.   What sort of a man is he!

MIN.   Big — very big — awfully big! Great big arms that carried me as if I were a feather; big beard, too; and it tickled me so when he — he pretended that he was my father.   And oh! I know I should be so awfully fond of him.   And oh, Kitty darling, what do you think?

KIT.   What, dearest?

MIN.   Why, I'm — I'm afraid — I'm really beginning to — to — like him — just a little tiny bit.

KIT.   Well, he sha'n't trouble you any more.

MIN.   But I *want* him to.

KIT.   Oh, nonsense, child!

A GAME OF CRIBBAGE.

By Charles Dickens.

CHARACTERS

Dick Swiveller.
The Marchioness.

(Dick Swiveller *discovered playing solitaire cribbage. Hearing a slight noise, he goes softly to the door, opens it, and pounces upon the* Marchioness, *who has been peeping through the keyhole.*)

The Marchioness. Oh! I didn't mean any harm; indeed, upon my word I didn't. (*Struggling.*) It's so very dull down-stairs. Please don't tell upon me; please don't!

Dick. Tell upon you! Do you mean to say you were looking through the keyhole for company?

March. Yes; upon my word I was.

Dick. How long have you been cooling your eye there?

March. Oh, ever since you began to play them cards, and long before.

Dick (*considering*). Well — come in. Here — sit down and I'll teach you how to play.

March. Oh! I durstn't do it; Miss Sally 'ud kill me, if she know'd I come up here.

Dick (*pulling her in by the arm*). Why, how thin you are! What do you mean by it?

March. It ain't my fault.

Dick. Could you eat any bread and meat? Yes? Ah! I thought so. Did you ever taste beer?

MARCH.   I had a sip of it once.

DICK.   Here's a state of things!   She *never* tasted it —
it can't be tasted in a sip!   Why, how old are you?

MARCH.   I don't know.

DICK (*setting before her a plate with bread and beef*).
There!   First of all clear that off, and then you'll see what's
next. . . .   Next (*giving her mug of beer*), take a pull at
that; but moderate your transports, you know, for you're
not used to it.   Well, is it good?

MARCH.   Oh! isn't it?

DICK (*putting sixpences into saucer, and dealing cards*).
Now, those are the stakes.   If you win, you get 'em all.   If
I win, I get 'em.   To make it seem more real and pleasant,
I shall call you the Marchioness; do you hear?   (MARCHION-
ESS *nods.*)   Then, Marchioness, fire away!   (*Starting to
play.*)   The Baron Sampsono Brasso and his fair sister are,
you tell me, at the play?   (MARCHIONESS *nods.*)   Ha!   'Tis
well, Marchioness! — but no matter.   Some wine there.
Ho!!   Marchioness, since life like a river is flowing, I care
not how fast it rolls on, ma'am, on, while such beer on the
bank still is growing, and such eyes light the waves as they
run.   Marchioness, your health.   You will excuse my wearing my hat, but the palace is damp, and the marble floor is
— if I may be allowed the expression — sloppy.   (*Becoming
less theatrical.*)   Do they often go where glory waits 'em, and
leave you here?

MARCH.   Oh, yes; I believe you they do; Miss Sally's
such a one-er for that, she is.

DICK.   Such a what?

MARCH.   Such a one-er.   They sometimes go to see Mr.
Quilp; they go to many places, bless you!

DICK.   Is Mr. Brass a wunner?

MARCH.   Not half what Miss Sally is, he isn't.   Bless
you! he'd never do anything without her.

DICK.   Oh!   He wouldn't, wouldn't he?

MARCH. Miss Sally keeps him in such order; he always asks her advice, he does! And he catches it sometimes. Bless you! you wouldn't believe how much he catches it.

DICK. I suppose that they consult together a good deal, and talk about a great many people — about me, for instance, sometimes, eh, Marchioness? (*She nods.*) Complimentary? (*Shakes her head violently.*) Humph! Would it be any breach of confidence, Marchioness, to relate what they say of the humble individual who has now the honor to — ?

MARCH. Miss Sally says you're a funny chap.

DICK. Well, Marchioness, that's not uncomplimentary. Merriment, Marchioness, is not a bad or degrading quality. Old King Cole was himself a merry old soul, if we may put any faith in the pages of history.

MARCH. But she says that you ain't to be trusted.

DICK. Why, really, Marchioness, several ladies and gentlemen — not exactly professional persons, but tradespeople, ma'am, tradespeople — have made the same remark. The obscure citizen who keeps the hotel over the way inclined strongly to that opinion to-night, when I ordered him to prepare the banquet. It's a popular prejudice, Marchioness, and yet I am sure I don't know why, for I have been trusted in my time to a considerable amount, and I can safely say that I never forsook my trust until it deserted me — never. Mr. Brass is of the same opinion, I suppose?

MARCH. (*nodding*). But don't you ever tell upon me, or I shall be beat to death.

DICK (*rising*). Marchioness, the word of a gentleman is as good as his bond — sometimes better, as in the present case, where his bond might prove but a doubtful sort of security. I am your friend, and I hope we shall play many more rubbers together in this same saloon. But, Marchioness, it occurs to me that you must be in the constant habit of airing your eye at keyholes, to know all this.

MARCH.   I only wanted to know where the key of the safe was hid; that was all; and I wouldn't have taken much, if I had found it — only enough to squench my hunger.

DICK.   You didn't find it, then?   But of course you didn't, or you'd be plumper.   Good-night, Marchioness.   Fare thee well, and if forever, then forever fare thee well.

TWO SCENES FROM "SQUIRE KATE."

BY ROBERT BUCHANAN.

CHARACTERS.

CATHERINE.
BRIDGET.

SCENE I.

THE SEPARATION.

CATHERINE. My God! what is it? what is this coming over me? It feels like death! He loves her — they love each other! Ah no, it can't be true. I won't believe it: it is too horrible; and yet I might have known it. I was too happy — it could not last. And *she*, my own sister, has come between us — she who was dearer to me than all the world. As she looked into his eyes, as his kisses fell upon her face, all my love was turned to hate; I could have *killed* her where she stood. No, no! not that I don't turn my heart against *her*, the little one for whom I would have given my life!

(CATHERINE *sits; enter* BRIDGET.)

BRIDGET. Catherine! What is the matter, Catherine? You are not well. (*Comes toward her.* CATHERINE *puts out her hand to keep her back.*)

CATH. I am not ill.

BRID. There is something the matter! Tell me what it is. Tell me why you left the dance and came here all alone.

(*Reprinted by permission of Lovell, Coryell & Co.*)

(CATHERINE *puts her hand to her head and moans.* BRIDGET *kneels beside her chair.*)   You *are* in trouble, Catherine, and you must tell me what it is, that I may help you!

CATH.   You help me?   *You!*

BRID.   Yes, dear; who has a better right?   Do not turn away from me, Catherine.   I want you to be tender to me to-night, for I — oh, it seems wicked to say it when you are so sad — I am so happy.   Listen, Catherine!   I want to tell you about George.   He loves me — he has told me he loves me!

CATH.   Why do you tell me what I know already?

BRID.   You know it? and you are glad!   O Catherine, tell me you are glad.

CATH.   *Glad?*   Yes, very glad.

BRID.   Catherine!   Catherine, you are angry with me; tell me why.   Perhaps you think I should have told you sooner; but indeed, I only heard it yesterday for the first. time, though of course I guessed.   Do you think I would have kept it from you — you who have always loved me, and whom I too have loved so much?

CATH.   Loved me?   You?

BRID.   Ah yes! and you know it; and indeed, it is because you have always liked him that I learned to love him. Don't think my love for him will ever change my heart toward *you*, Catherine.   You will always be the same to me, my sister — my own dear sister.   Catherine, you are crying! What is it?   Won't you tell me, dear?   (*Puts arm around her, but is pushed aside.*)

CATH. (*rising*).   Don't touch me!   Don't speak to me! Go, and leave me to myself!

BRID.   But you are in trouble!   Something has happened.

CATH.   Nothing, nothing!

BRID.   You're not angry with me?

CATH.   *Why* won't you leave me?   Why do you torture me with your presence?   I tell you I am sick to death of all the world. Everything is false, even those we care for most! This is how we are punished! We give our lives away for others; we sacrifice ourselves for them; we toil and suffer for their happiness, and they reward us with treachery and lies!

BRID. I have never lied or been treacherous to you, Catherine. I have always loved you.

CATH. It's false! You have never loved me. I have reared you as if you were my own child; I have worked and slaved, and all for you, — and now what is my reward? But there! that is all over; I'll work and slave no more for them that scorn me. I am rich now. I can rest; it will be your turn now. Yes, you, the fine lady, will have to work now and earn your bread!

BRID. Catherine! Catherine! What are you saying? Why are you so bitter against me — you who have always been so kind?

CATH. Ah, yes! you can cry now, and pretend not to understand, but you can't deceive me; I'm past that. You have plotted and plotted, smiled and coquetted, to win his heart, and never said one word to me. But don't tell me again that he cares for you — don't! unless you wish to drive me mad.

BRID. But *why?* You have always liked him too!

CATH. It is false! I have always *hated* him! I hate him still. But *you* sha'n't marry him! You *cannot.* He has nothing — you have nothing! You shall never marry him — never — never! (BRIDGET *looks at* CATHERINE *in amazement and terror.*)

BRID. O Catherine, forgive me, dear, forgive me! I did not understand; but I see now how blind I have been. *You* — you care for him?

CATH. And if I do? Have I no right to do that? Am I so coarse and common that I'm only the dust beneath his feet? You're a dainty lady, and I am only the drudge, the breadwinner; but if your skin is white, and men think you pretty, it's because I'm tanned with the sun and coarsened with wind and rain. If I am despised and thought common, it's because I've given all my life and my youth to make you what you are!

BRID. O Catherine, I know that! (*Coming toward her.*) Do you think I can ever forget it — my sister?

CATH. I am not your sister! Henceforth I am nothing to you; do you hear? Nothing! Our lives have been together, but from to-night they part. You can go your way, I will go mine. Yes, go after your lover. Take the way he took — leave my house! Go before you make me worse than I am — go, or — (*Raises her hand to strike;* BRIDGET *utters scream, and sinks on the floor.*)

BRID. Catherine! my own Catherine!

CATH. Out of my sight! I hate you! I hate him! I hate everything in the world!

BRID. Don't be so cruel! Don't speak to me so harshly! You know I never meant to harm you, and you will forgive me!

CATH. Never, never, never! You have poisoned my life and hardened my heart. There's nothing left now but hatred — yes, hatred, and most of all for you. Go! and never come back to me! Go! and never let me see your face again!

SCENE II.

THE REUNION.

CATHERINE. Bridget, I want to speak with you. You asked me last night what Geoffrey had said to me that had overcome me so. I am going to tell you, dear. You must be brave, for what I am going to tell you is terrible. Somebody has tried to kill you — to *poison* you, my child!

BRIDGET. Catherine!

CATH. And do you know who they say has done so? Do you know who is thought guilty of planning your death? Me!—your sister! (BRIDGET *throws herself into* CATHERINE'S *arms, and breaks into tears.*) You know it couldn't be!

BRID. Know it! Whoever said it?—whoever thought of such a wicked thing? My darling! My own dear Catherine! The sister who loved me, reared me, cheered me! Oh, shameful! cruel! Oh, don't think I believe it, dear!—don't, or it will kill me! But *some one* wished my death! Some one!

CATH. No one; no one. No one wished it, so don't talk of it. It's all a mistake. It has had its uses. It has brought us together again, little one. Let us forget it.

BRID. But why did they speak of poison? Why did they suspect you? Ah! I know—because of George. (CATHERINE *tries to speak, but* BRIDGET *stops her.*) No, no; don't speak yet. They think George came between us. They think we hate each other enough for a crime like that! And if you had been ill and dying they might have thought the same of *me*. Shame on them! Shame! But we'll silence them, dear; we'll stop their wicked tongues. We'll prove to them we are not so evil as they think us. We'll show them what we are to one another. You love George—you shall marry him.

CATH. Bridget! What are you saying? You would give him up to me?

BRID. You've given up all else in the world for my sake. You've given me all—your love, your life. It's my turn now.

CATH. And yet you love him.

BRID. No, no; at least, I can forget him.

CATH. Could you ever do that, little one?

BRID. Ye-es. I would try. I must! I will!

CATH. No, no! You're too weak, my darling, too like a tender flower. You'd droop and die without George's love. You shall not.

BRID. But you — you? Oh, it's shameful — I can do nothing — give nothing, and you have given me all. I won't marry George. I'd rather die!

CATH. Hush, dear! and let me speak. It was just madness and folly on my part; it was only a day's shadow on our lives. I thought I loved George — I thought he might have learned to love me. No, little one; I was mad, and God has brought me back my reason. It's you, not I, that must be George's wife. And now all we have to do is to call the happy man and name the day, and set the bells a-ringing. Not a word, little one! It shall be as I say. You shall marry your own true love, and soon, soon! You won't forget me in your happiness, will you, dear? Nay, nay, dear, you mustn't cry yourself ill again. We'll forget all our troubles. There'll be nothing but sunshine and merrymaking now. A wedding-dress for my little sister, a wedding-dress!

SCENE FROM "KENILWORTH."

BY SIR WALTER SCOTT.

CHARACTERS.

QUEEN ELIZABETH.
AMY ROBSART.

(QUEEN ELIZABETH *is visiting the castle of her favorite, Lord Leicester. Leaving her train in the grounds, she retires to a grotto, where she finds* AMY ROBSART, *who has been secretly wedded to Leicester, and who was then a prisoner of Varney, an attendant of Leicester. She escaped from him to seek protection from the* QUEEN.)

ELIZABETH. How now, fair nymph of this lovely grotto! Art spell-bound and struck with dumbness by the charms of the wicked enchanter Fear? We are his sworn enemy, maiden, and can reverse his charm. Speak, we command thee. (AMY *drops on her knee before the* QUEEN, *clasps her hands, and looks up supplicatingly.*) What may this mean? This is a stronger passion than befits the occasion. Stand up, damsel! (AMY *rises.*) What wouldst thou have with us?

AMY. Your protection, madam.

ELIZ. Each daughter of England has it while she is worthy of it; but your distress seems to have a deeper root than a forgotten task. Why, and in what, do you crave our protection?

AMY (*hesitating*). Alas! I know not.

ELIZ. This is folly, maiden. The sick must tell his malady to the physician; nor are we accustomed to ask questions so oft, without receiving an answer.

95

AMY.   I request — I implore — I beseech your gracious
protection — against — against one Varney.

ELIZ.   What Varney? — Sir Richard Varney — the servant of Lord Leicester?   What, damsel, are you to him, or
he to you?

AMY.   I — I — was his prisoner — and he practised on
my life, and I broke forth to — to —

ELIZ.   To throw yourself on my protection, doubtless.
Thou shalt have it — that is, if thou art worthy; for we will
sift this matter to the uttermost.   Thou art — (*looking at her
intently*) thou art Amy, daughter of Sir Hugh Robsart of
Lidcote Hall?

AMY (*drops on her knee again*).   Forgive me — forgive me
most gracious princess!

ELIZ.   For what should I forgive thee, silly wench? for
being the daughter of thine own father?   Thou art brain-
sick, surely.   Well, I see I must wring the story from thee
by inches.   Thou didst deceive thine old and honored father
— thy look confesses it — cheated Master Tressilian —
thy blush avouches it — and married this same Varney.

AMY (*springing to her feet*).   No, madam; no!   As there is
a God above us, I am not the sordid wretch you would
make me.   I am not the wife of that contemptible slave of
— of that most deliberate villain!   I am not the wife of
Varney.   I would rather be the bride of Destruction.

ELIZ.   Why, God ha' mercy, woman!   I see thou canst
talk fast enough when the theme likes thee.   Nay, tell me
woman, tell me — for by God's day, I *will* know — whose
wife or whose paramour art thou?   Speak out, and be
speedy.   Thou wert better dally with a lioness than with
Elizabeth.

AMY (*despairingly*).   The Earl of Leicester knows it all.

ELIZ.   The Earl of Leicester!   The Earl of Leicester!
Woman thou art set on to this — thou dost belie him —
he takes no keep of such as thou art.   Thou art suborned

to slander the noblest lord and the truest-hearted gentleman in England.   But were he the right of our trust, or
something yet dearer to us, thou shalt have thy hearing,
and that in his presence.   Come with me — come with me
instantly !

SCENE FROM "VANITY FAIR."

By Wm. Makepeace Thackeray.

CHARACTERS.

Rebecca Sharp.
Miss Crawley.
Sir Pitt.

(Miss Crawley *seated reading a novel;* Rebecca Sharp *gazing out of the window.*)

Rebecca (*alarmed*). Here's Sir Pitt, ma'am! (*Knock heard from outside.*)

Miss Crawley (*going out*). My dear, I can't see him. I won't see him. Tell him not at home, or say I'm too ill to receive any one. My nerves won't bear my brother at this moment. (*Exit. Enter* Sir Pitt.)

Reb. (*to* Sir Pitt). She's too ill to see you, sir.

Sir Pitt. So much the better; I wawnt to see *you*, Miss Becky. (*Taking off his hat and gloves.*) I wawnt you back at Queen's Crawley, Miss.

Reb. I hope to come soon, as soon as dear Miss Crawley is better — and return to — to the dear children.

Sir P. You've said so these three months, Becky, and still you go hanging on to my sister, who'll fling you off like an old shoe, when she's wore you out. I tell you I *want* you. I'm going back to Queen's Crawley. Will you come back? Yes or no.

Reb. I daren't — I don't think — it would be right — to be alone — with you, sir.

Sir P. (*thumping the table*). I say agin, I want you. I

can't git on without you. I didn't see what it was till you went away. The house all goes wrong. It's not the same place. All my accounts has got muddled agin. You *must* come back. Do come back. Dear Becky, do come!

REB. Come — as what, sir?

SIR P. Come as Lady Crawley if you like. There! will that satusfy you? Come back and be my wife. You're vit vor't. Birth be hanged! You're as good a lady as ever I see. You've got more brains in your little vinger than any baronet's wife in the country. Will you come? Yes, or no?

REB. Oh, Sir Pitt!

SIR P. Say yes, Becky. I'm an old man, but a good'n. I'm good for twenty years. I'll make you happy, see if I don't. You shall do what you like, and 'av it all your own way. I'll make you a zettlement. I'll do everything regular. (*Falling on his knees.*) Look year!

REB. O Sir Pitt! Oh, sir — I — I'm *married already.*

SIR P. (*bouncing up*). Married! You're joking. You're making vun of me, Becky. Who'd ever go to marry you without a shilling to your vortune?

REB. (*in an agony of tears*). Married! married! O Sir Pitt! dear Sir Pitt, do not think me ungrateful for all your goodness to me. It is only your generosity that has extorted my secret.

SIR P. Generosity be hanged! Who is it to, then, you're married? Where was it?

REB. Let me come back with you to the country, sir! Let me watch over you as faithfully as ever! Don't, don't separate me from dear Queen's Crawley!

SIR P. The feller has left you, has he? Well, Becky, come back if you like. You can't eat your cake and have it. Anyways, I made you a vair offer. Come back as governess — you shall have it all your own way. (BECKY *still weeping and holding out one hand.*) So the rascal ran off, eh? (*Consolingly.*)   Never mind, Becky; *I'll* take care of 'ee.

REB.   Oh, sir, it would be the pride of my life to go back to Queen's Crawley, and take care of the children and of you as formerly, when you said you were pleased with the services of your little Rebecca.   When I think of what you have just offered me, my heart fills with gratitude — indeed it does !   I can't be your wife, sir ; let me — let me be your daughter !   (REBECCA *falls on her knees, looks up in his face pathetically, when* MISS CRAWLEY *opens the door and walks in.*)

MISS C.   It is the lady on the ground, and not the gentle-man.   They told me that *you* were on your knees, Sir Pitt; do kneel once more, and let me see this pretty couple !

REB.   I have thanked Sir Pitt Crawley, ma'am (*rising*), and have told him that — that I never can become **Lady** Crawley.

MISS C.   Refused him !

REB.   Yes — refused.

MISS C.   And am I to credit my ears that you absolutely proposed to her, Sir Pitt?

SIR P.   Ees, I did.

MISS C.   And she refused you, as she says?

SIR P.   Ees.

MISS C.   It does not seem to break your heart, at any rate ?

SIR P.   Nawt a bit.   (*Laughing.*)

MISS C.   I'm glad you think it good sport, brother.

SIR P.   Vamous.   Who'd ha' thought it ! what a shy little devil ! what a little fox it waws !

MISS C. (*stamping her foot*).   Who'd have thought what ? Pray, Miss Sharp, are you waiting for the Prince Regent's divorce, that you don't think our family good enough for you ?

REB.   My attitude when you came in, ma'am, did **not**

look as if I despised such an honor as this good — this noble man has deigned to offer me. Do you think I have no heart? Have you all loved me and been kind to the poor orphan-deserted-girl, and am I to feel nothing? O my friends! O my benefactors! may not my love, my life, my duty, try to repay the confidence you have shown me? Do you grudge me even gratitude, Miss Crawley? It is too much — my heart is too full. (*Sinking in chair.*)

Sir P. Whether you marry me or not, you're a good girl, Becky, and I'm your vriend, mind. (*Exit.*)

Miss C. Well, my dear, who is it? You never would have refused him had there not been some one else in the case. Tell me the private reasons. There *is* some one; who is it that has touched your heart?

Reb. You have guessed right, dear lady. You wonder at one so poor and friendless having an attachment, don't you? I have never heard that poverty was any safeguard against it. I wish it were.

Miss C. My poor, dear child! Are we pining in secret? Tell me all, and let me console you.

Reb. I wish you could. Indeed, indeed, I need it. (*Laying her head on* Miss Crawley's *shoulder.*) Don't ask me now. You shall know all soon. Dear, kind Miss Crawley — dear friend, may I say so?

Miss C. That you may, my child. I don't intend to let you stir for years, you may depend upon it. As for going back to that odious brother of mine, after what has passed, it is out of the question. You must stay and take care of the old woman.

COMEDY SKETCHES

By Julian Sturgis

A collection of short plays suited for amateur theatricals or high-class vaudeville, easy to produce and of high quality. Recommended especially for parlor performance.

CONTENTS

APPLES. One male, one female.
FIRE FLIES. One male, one female.
HEATHER. One male, one female.
PICKING UP THE PIECES. One male, one female.
HALF-WAY TO ARCADY. One male, one female.
MABEL'S HOLY DAY. Two males, one female.
Twenty minutes each.
Price, 25 cents

IN OFFICE HOURS

And Other Sketches

By Evelyn Greenleaf Sutherland

CONTENTS

IN OFFICE HOURS. Comedy Sketch in One Act, five males, four females.

A QUILTING PARTY IN THE THIRTIES. Outline Sketch for Music, six males, four females, and chorus.

IN AUNT CHLOE'S CABIN. Negro Comedy Sketch in One Act, seventeen female characters and "supers."

THE STORY OF A FAMOUS WEDDING. Outline Sketch for Music and Dancing, six males, four females.
Price, 25 cents

THE SOUP TUREEN

And Other Duologues

A collection of short plays for two and three characters. Good quality, high tone and confidently offered to the best taste.

CONTENTS

THE SOUP TUREEN. One male, two females.
LELIA. One male, one female.
THE UNLUCKY STAR. Two males.
THE SERENADE. Two females.
Play twenty minutes each.
Price, 25 cents

HOLIDAY DIALOGUES FROM DICKENS

Arranged by W. E. Fette

Comprising selections from "The Christmas Carol," "The Cricket on the Hearth," "The Battle of Life," etc., arranged in a series of scenes to be given either singly or together, as an extended entertainment. For the celebration of Christmas no better material can be found.
Price, 25 cents

THE CRIMSON COCOANUT

And Other Plays

By Ian Hay

This collection contains the following titles, all of which can be confidently recommended for amateur performance in schools or elsewhere as high in tone and exceptionally amusing. Mr. Hay is well known as a novelist and literary man.

THE CRIMSON COCOANUT

An Absurdity in One Act. Four males, two females. Costumes, modern; scenery, an interior. Plays thirty-five minutes. Mr. Pincher, of Scotland Yard, in pursuit of some dangerous anarchists, entangles the lady of his choice and her father in some humorous perils, but ends by capturing both the criminals and the lady. Author's royalty of $5.00 for amateur performance.

A LATE DELIVERY

A Play in Three Episodes. Three males, two females. Scene, an interior; costumes, modern. Plays forty minutes. Bill, a middle-aged admirer of Marjorie, learns just as he has finished a letter to her proposing marriage that Tim, a young man, is also in love with her. He assumes her to love his rival and does not mail the letter. She finds it on his desk and opens it, and learning the truth makes choice of the older and better man. Royalty for amateurs, $5.00 for each performance.

THE MISSING CARD

A Comedietta in One Act. Two males, two females. Scene, an interior; costumes, modern. Plays thirty minutes. Two elderly admirers of Mrs. Millington decide to deal the pack to see which shall first propose to her, the one who gets the Queen of Hearts to win. She privately takes this card out of the pack and when they have gone through it in vain, announces her engagement to another man. Royalty for amateurs, $5.00 a performance.

Price, all three in one volume, 50 cents

THE MARRIAGE OF JACK AND JILL

A Mother Goose Entertainment in Two Scenes

By Lilian Clisby Bridgham

Forty children. Costumes, wedding; no scenery required. Plays forty minutes. A Mother Goose wedding and reception carried out by the smallest children. Very pretty and easy to get up; strongly recommended. Not a pantomime merely, but calls for some speaking parts.

Price, 25 cents

LOST—A CHAPERON

A Comedy in Three Acts by Courtney Bruerton and W. S. Maulsby. Six male, nine female characters. Costumes, modern; scenery, an interior and an exterior. Plays a full evening. A lot of college girls in camp lose their chaperon for twenty-four hours, and are provided by a camp of college boys across the lake with plenty of excitement. The parts are all good, the situations are very funny and the lines full of laughs. Recommended for high-school performance. *Price, 25 cents*

THE PRIVATE TUTOR

A Farce in Three Acts by E. J. Whisler. Five male, three female characters. Costumes, modern; scenery, two simple interiors. Plays two hours. Tells of the endeavors of two college boys to disguise the fact that they have been "rusticated" from the family of one of them. Hans Dinklederfer, the leader of a German band, trying to make good in the character of a private tutor, is a scream. All the parts are good. A capital high-school play. *Price, 25 cents*

THE REBELLION OF MRS. BARCLAY

A Comedy of Domestic Life in Two Acts by May E. Countryman. Three male, six female characters. Costumes, modern; scenery, easy interiors. Plays one hour and three-quarters. A clever and amusing comedy with all the parts evenly good. There are many Mr. Barclays all over this country, and Mrs. Barclay's method of curing her particular one will be sympathetically received. Good Irish comedy parts, male and female. Strongly recommended. *Price, 25 cents*

THE TRAMPS' CONVENTION

An Entertainment in One Scene for Male Characters Only by Jessie A. Kelley. Seventeen male characters. Costumes, typical tramp dress; scenery, unimportant. Plays an hour and a half. An entertainment in the vaudeville class, with possibilities of unlimited fun. Music can be introduced, if desired, though this is not necessary. The opening is very funny and original and the finish—The Ananias Club—can be worked up to any extent. Strongly recommended. *Price, 25 cents*

THE DAY THAT LINCOLN DIED

A Play in One Act by Prescott Warren and Will Hutchins. Five male, two female characters. Costumes, modern; scene, an easy exterior. Plays thirty minutes. A very effective play suited for a Lincoln Day entertainment. It offers plenty of comedy, and is a piece that we can heartily recommend. Professional stage-rights reserved. *Price, 25 cents*

PA'S NEW HOUSEKEEPER

A Farce in One Act by Charles S. Bird. Three male, two female characters. Modern costumes; scenery, a simple interior or none at all. Plays forty minutes. Jack Brown, visiting his chum, is tempted by his success in college theatricals to make up in the character of the new housekeeper, an attractive widow, who is expected but does not arrive. He takes in everybody and mixes things up generally. All the parts are first rate and the piece full of laughs. Strongly recommended. *Price, 15 cents*

THE TIME OF HIS LIFE

A Comedy in Three Acts by C. Leona Dalrymple. Six males, three females. Costumes, modern; scenery, two interiors, or can be played in one. Plays two hours and a half. A side-splitting piece, full of action and a sure success if competently acted. Tom Carter's little joke of impersonating the colored butler has unexpected consequences that give him "the time of his life." Very highly recommended for high school performance. *Price, 25 cents*

THE COLLEGE CHAP

A Comedy Drama in Three Acts by Harry L. Newton and John Pierre Roche. Eleven males, seven females. Costumes, modern; scenery, two interiors. Plays two and a half hours. An admirable play for amateurs. Absolutely American in spirit and up to date; full of sympathetic interest but plenty of comedy; lots of healthy sentiment, but nothing "mushy." Just the thing for high schools; sane, effective, and not difficult. *Price, 25 cents*

THE DEACON'S SECOND WIFE

A Comedy in Three Acts by Allan Abbott. Six males, six females. Costumes, modern; scenery, one interior, one exterior. Plays two hours and a half. A play of rural life specially written for school performance. All the parts are good and of nearly equal opportunity, and the piece is full of laughs. Easy to produce; no awkward sentimental scenes; can be strongly recommended for high schools. *Price, 25 cents*

THE TEASER

A Rural Comedy in Three Acts by Charles S. Allen. Four male, three female characters. Scene, an easy interior, the same for all three acts; costumes, modern. Plays an hour and a half. An admirable play for amateurs, very easy to get up, and very effective. Uraliah Higgins, a country postman, and Drusilla Todd are capital comedy parts, introducing songs or specialties, if desired. Plenty of incidental fun. *Price, 25 cents*

COUNTRY FOLKS

A Comedy Drama in Three Acts by Anthony E. Wills. Six males, five females. Costumes, modern; scenery, one interior. Plays two and a quarter hours. An effective and up-to-date play well suited for amateur performance. All the parts good and fairly even in point of opportunity; the ladies' parts especially so. Easy to stage, and well suited for schools. Well recommended. *Price, 25 cents*

THE MISHAPS OF MINERVA

A Farce in Two Acts by Bertha Currier Porter. Five males, eight females. Costumes, modern; scene, an interior. Plays one and a half hours. An exceptionally bright and amusing little play of high class and recommended to all classes of amateur players. Full of action and laughs, but refined. Irish low comedy part. Strongly endorsed. *Price, 25 cents*

THE VILLAGE POST-OFFICE

An Entertainment in One Scene by Jessie A. Kelley. Twenty-two males and twenty females are called for, but one person may take several parts and some characters may be omitted. The stage is arranged as a country store and post-office in one. Costumes are rural and funny. Plays a full evening. Full of " good lines " and comical incident and character. Strongly recommended for church entertainments or general use ; very wholesome and clean. *Price, 25 cents*

MISS FEARLESS & CO.

A Comedy in Three Acts by Belle Marshall Locke. Ten females. Scenery, two interiors ; costumes, modern. Plays a full evening. A bright and interesting play full of action and incident. Can be strongly recommended. All the parts are good. Sarah Jane Lovejoy, Katie O'Connor and Euphemia Addison are admirable character parts, and Miss Alias and Miss Alibi, the " silent sisters," offer a side-splitting novelty. *Price, 25 cents*

LUCIA'S LOVER

A Farce in Three Acts by Bertha Currier Porter. Eight females. Costumes, modern ; scenery, two interiors. Plays an hour and a half. A bright and graceful piece, light in character, but sympathetic and amusing. Six contrasted types of girls at boarding-school are shown in a novel story. Lots of fun, but very refined. Easy to produce and can be strongly recommended. *Price, 25 cents*

A GIRL IN A THOUSAND

A Comedy in Four Acts by Evelyn Gray Whiting. Fourteen females. Costumes, modern ; scenes, three interiors and an exterior. Plays a full evening. Very strong and sympathetic and of varied interest. Irish comedy; strong " witch " character; two very lively " kids "; all the parts good. Effective, easy to produce, and can be strongly recommended as thoroughly wholesome in tone as well as amusing. *Price, 25 cents*

MRS. BRIGGS OF THE POULTRY YARD

A Comedy in Three Acts by Evelyn Gray Whiting. Four males, seven females. Scene, an interior ; costumes, modern. A domestic comedy looking steadfastly at the " bright side " of human affairs. Mrs. Briggs is an admirable part, full of original humor and quaint sayings, and all the characters are full of opportunity. Simply but effectively constructed, and written with great humor. Plays two hours. *Price, 25 cents*

TOMMY'S WIFE

A Farce in Three Acts by Marie J. Warren. Three males, five females. Costumes, modern ; scenery, two interiors. Plays an hour and a half. Originally produced by students of Wellesley College. A very original and entertaining play, distinguished by abundant humor. An unusually clever piece, strongly recommended. *Price, 25 cents*

THE ELOPEMENT OF ELLEN

A Farce Comedy in Three Acts by Marie J. Warren. Four males, three females. Costumes, modern; scenery, one interior and one exterior. Plays an hour and a half. A bright and ingenious little play, admirably suited for amateur acting. Written for and originally produced by Wellesley College girls. Strongly recommended.

Price, 25 cents

A VIRGINIA HEROINE

A Comedy in Three Acts by Susie G. McGlone. Eleven female characters. Scenery, easy; costumes, modern. Plays one hour and forty-five minutes. Irish and Negro comedy parts, and two character parts; most of the characters young. A very easy and interesting play for girls, well suited for school performance. Romantic interest with lots of comedy.

Price, 25 cents

OUR CHURCH FAIR

A Farcical Entertainment in Two Acts by Jessie A. Kelley. Twelve females. Costumes, modern; scenery, unimportant. Plays an hour and a quarter. A humorous picture of the planning of the annual church fair by the ladies of the sewing circle. Full of local hits and general human nature, and a sure laugh-producer in any community. Can be recommended. *Price, 25 cents*

ALL CHARLEY'S FAULT

A Farce in Two Acts by Anthony E. Wills. Six males, three females. Scenery, an easy interior; costumes, modern. Plays two hours. A very lively and laughable piece, full of action and admirably adapted for amateur performance. Dutch and Negro comedy characters. Plays very rapidly with lots of incident and not a dull moment. Strongly recommended. *Price, 15 cents*

HOW THE STORY GREW

An Entertainment for Women's Clubs in One Act by O. W. Gleason. Eight female characters. Costumes, modern; scenery, unimportant; may be given on a platform without any. Plays forty-five minutes. A very easy and amusing little piece, full of human nature and hitting off a well-known peculiarity of almost any community. Written for middle-aged women, and a sure hit with the audience. *Price, 15 cents*

THE COUNTRY DOCTOR

A Comedy Drama in Four Acts by Arthur Lewis Tubbs. Six males, five females. Costumes, modern; scenery, two interiors. Plays two hours. Easy to stage and full of interest. The female parts are the stronger, being exceptionally good. Negro and " hayseed " comedy parts. A very strong dramatic piece. Can be recommended. *Price, 25 cents*

Breinigsville, PA USA
21 March 2011
258075BV00003B/4/P